Growth and Life in the Local Church

Growth
and Life
in the
Local
Church

H. BOONE PORTER, JR.

William Carey Library

SOUTH PASADENA, CALIF.

Library of Congress Cataloging in Publication Data

Porter, Henry Boone, 1923-
   Growth and life in the local church.

   Originally presented (chapters 1, 3, 4, and 5) as
McMath lectures in the Diocese of Michigan.
   Includes bibliographical references.
   1. Church renewal.   2. Pastoral theology.
I. Title.
BV4011.P6 1974   262'.001   73-19847
ISBN 0-87808-141-0

The substance of chapters 1, 3, 4, and 5
of *Growth and Life in the Local Church*
was originally presented as McMath Lectures
in the Diocese of Michigan

Address all orders to the
William Carey Library
533 Hermosa Street
South Pasadena, Calif. 91030

To Nicholas
(who is very young)

CONTENTS

PREFACE

The Church is a very old institution. It is far older than the American Government, or the public school system, or the language which we speak. It is vastly older than the customs, utensils, and media of communication which characterize our modern life. More than anything else with which most of us are familiar, the Christian Church is ancient.

Yet the Church is also the assembly of the firstborn; it is a joyful mother of children; it is the living temple of the God who makes all things new. Down through the ages, even in the most unlikely times and places, the Church has experienced renewal, and it has brought new life to men and women and children. Its essential and most characteristic acts are the proclamation of good news, the washing of a new birth, and the banquet of a new covenant. The Church watches and waits, but it does so in order to proclaim a new day to the human race.

Most of us can recall an era when the age, stability, and continuity of the Church seemed to be its most precious and inviting characteristics. In a rapidly changing world, an unchanging Church stood not only for security, but also for dignity, for wisdom, and a human heritage which the recently invented machine must not destroy. Now in a remarkably short time, we have learned to live at a rapid pace, and we have learned that the Church can move very rapidly too. God has given us the privilege of living in an age of extraordinary discoveries and opportunities. In such an age the Church must be nimble, adventurous, and youthful. "Christian renewal" has become the watchword of church leaders everywhere.

Christian renewal may be experienced by individuals and by congregations in many ways, but it is not so easily defined. Many indeed would maintain that the revitalization of the Church in our time requires quite specific resistance to the custom of those theologians and historians who wish to encircle every phenomenon with precise definitions. Some would identify renewal very closely with the present and personal experience of St. Paul's intuition that "the letter killeth, but the spirit giveth life" (II Corinthians 3:6). Some aspects of reality do indeed evade definition, yet we must, nonetheless, seek to consider them and understand them as best as we can. The new life appearing in the Church today is not only a challenge to our commitment and devotion; it is also a challenge to our minds, to our foresight, to our willingness to apply our talents wisely in the years ahead.

Many aspects of Christian renewal have in fact been carefully studied and ably written about. The ecumenical movement, the liturgical movement, and the revival of biblical theology have stimulated a large and growing literature. New ethical, educational, sociological, and philosophical problems are also being considered by creative Christian thinkers today. Yet one very basic and fundamental aspect of the renewal of the Church has been largely ignored: the question of the growth of the Christian community, that is, the ability of the Church to relate its ministry to the vast numbers of people who live in our nation and every other nation today. If Christian renewal is to be a continuing and effective force, then those who are committed to renewal must bring their talents and distinctive insights to bear on such questions as evangelism, the founding of new congregations and parishes, and the enrollment of sufficient persons to do the things which need to be done in a growing Christian community.

The existence of this problem on a national and international scale is, one hopes, obvious to every thinking and responsible person. The bearing of this problem on the local situation is in fact just as urgent but far less obvious. Those of us who sit on the Home Mission boards of denominational and interdenominational bodies know well how much confusion of thought reigns. Very few clear efforts have been made to explain to the ordinary middle-class American Christian just how and why the extension of the Church and the expansion of its ministry must affect him, his family, and the local congregation of which he is a member. This is the topic with which the present volume is concerned. This book is not primarily concerned with new questions of theology, education, or social witness but, rather, with the vitality and growth of the Christian community itself, without which Christian thought and Christian action can scarcely exist.

The first chapters will accordingly consider the capacity of churches to attract new members and to incorporate them into the Body of Christ. This leads inevitably to the question of providing enough parishes, and enough pastoral care, for ever-growing numbers of people. Because these are matters not just for speculation but for practical action, a concrete case history has been offered in some detail in Chapter 4. This has provided a welcome opportunity to assemble the history of a very interesting, but hitherto unrecorded, episode in modern American church history. Because the growth of the Church must be inspired by God and directed to serve his purposes, a chapter has been devoted to the prayers, sacraments, and forms of worship by which Christians invoke God's Spirit and dedicate themselves to Christ. Because the weekly assembly of people for worship is the most evident and visible action of the ordinary parish in the ordinary round of local life, this topic is of major concern for any effective Christian strategy. The concluding chapter deals with methods and procedures for implementing at the present time some of the principles discussed in this book.

Most of the problems and questions to be discussed are equally relevant for almost all Christian churches in America at the present time, and it is well to be aware of this. The author is a priest of the Episcopal Church, and refers most readily to examples within the life of his own church. At the same time, references to situations in other churches are deliberately included. The making of comparisons across denominational boundaries is frequently instructive to all concerned. We can often understand our own strengths and weaknesses better when we see them in slightly different terms and circumstances. The kinds of questions to be discussed here have, from the very outset, been studied in ecumenical terms, and they should continue to be.

It is a pleasure to express my gratitude to the many persons who have had a share in bringing this book to fruition. Above all, my thanks are due to Mr. and Mrs. Neil C. McMath of Bloomfield Hills, Michigan, the generous founders of the McMath Lectureship. The substance of Chapters 1, 3, 4, and 5 was presented as McMath Lectures in Detroit in November of 1965. I am likewise much indebted to the Right Rev. Richard S. Emrich, Ph.D., Bishop of Michigan, and the Rev. G. Burton Hodgson for their generous help and assistance. The encouragement and hospitality of the many clergy and lay people of Michigan who constituted the audience of the McMath Lectures are also gratefully remembered. Without the interest and cooperation of a large number of persons who helped me with research in southwestern Indiana, Chapter 4 could never have been written. I much appreciate the time and attention which they gave. Fuller acknowledgment of the assistance of particular individuals is recorded in the notes to that chapter. Mrs. Ann M.

Saums is to be thanked for carefully copying and recopying this material. Finally, in this as in so much else, my thanks are due to my wife, Violet M. Porter, for her considerable help in the writing of these pages.

1

CHURCH GROWTH TODAY

In considering the rejuvenation of the Christian life in the twentieth century, some may be surprised that we begin by giving our attention directly to church growth. This may seem a rather pragmatic point at which to start. Yet the first and most obvious characteristic of youth is the capacity for growth. A newly sprouted seedling, or a newly born suckling, can grow with extraordinary speed. If this capacity for growth is thwarted, the young organism will die. This is true in the sphere of biology, and it is also often true in the sphere of sociology. A newly organized band of people, animated with enthusiasm and hope, usually finds it easy to assimilate new members. Then, in order to continue to exist, any society or association must actively endeavor to attain *a sufficient membership to fulfill and implement its basic purposes.*

This latter principle appears to be a more inexorable law than the first. In order to make this point quite clear, it will be well to consider a specific illustration. A newly founded political club or party can quickly grow from a few dozen to a few hundred adherents. If it cannot attain a sufficient size to have any success, or foreseeable success, at the polls, the party will soon disperse and disband, for it will be unable to fulfill purposes for which it exists. If in fact it does not go out of existence after repeated and hopeless defeats, one will be forced to conclude that the purposes of the organization have undergone a tacit, and perhaps quite unconscious, transformation. If people continue to belong to a political club which never elects its candidates, it is probably because certain personal, professional, or intellectual associations within the party have in fact become more precious than the political aims to which the organization is nominally dedicated. Perhaps membership has prestige value: it is very easy to become an officer in a small group. Or perhaps membership in a dormant party presents an easy option to persons who are committed to lofty principles but who would be at a loss to implement them if they had the effective power to do so. Or perhaps older people belong simply because they enjoy the memory of the youthful enthusiasm which drew them into the organization many years before. In such a situation, a combination of several such factors can be expected to operate.

In this example, we should notice that this change of motivation does not necessarily involve moral turpitude. The desire to associate with friends, the enjoyment of memories, and pride in the discharge of small responsibilities are not evil motives. To some extent, they may be necessary in any large organization. In a purely social club these may quite properly be the main motives for membership. In the case of a political party, however, these secondary motives—if they achieve a primary place—may subvert the proper political aims for which the organization was founded. In the case of a small political group which perennially fails to win elections, this is what happens. Small sums of money are raised, petty officials are chosen, and little meetings are held —precisely because some people enjoy collecting money, being appointed to committees, and attending meetings.

In much the same way, an educational institution which fails to relate itself to new types of students will soon defect from its proper academic and intellectual goals. A business which cannot meet the needs of new consumers, or an orchestra which does not seek to attract new audiences, or an athletic team which does not seek new opponents—all of these will find, in their respective spheres, that their original commitments are gradually being lost sight of. If the organization continues to exist, it will be because a shift of motivation has taken place. They will doubtless continue to pay lip-service to their original purpose, but in fact the static organization is dominated by a different purpose—the desire of congenial people to associate with each other in a habitual manner which does not challenge their abilities too sharply. As with the political party which ceases to win elections, it holds the interest of persons who enjoy collecting small sums of money, being assigned to positions of nominal responsibility, and attending meetings.

The Christian Church was founded on a different basis, and continues its life for purposes quite different from those of the other types of organizations which we have mentioned. Nonetheless, this question of shifting motivation still arises. In fact we see religious bodies busy erecting large buildings, employing clerical and lay officials, and holding all sorts of meetings and assemblies. Yet they often seem strangely unconcerned about winning people to support the lofty goals to which their organizations are committed. In short, there is indeed evidence that church bodies, no less than secular societies and organizations, can lose sight of their professed objectives when they become static at a certain size and cease to grow. The maintenance of existing institutional structures, the perpetuation of agreeable personal relationships, and the reaffirmations of ideals which no longer threaten or challenge those who affirm them—these become the primary (though perhaps tacit) objectives of a church which cannot or will not grow.

Roland Allen, Twentieth-Century Prophet

The study of church growth thus involves the use of various kinds of sociological data in the effort to meet evangelistic, moral, and spiritual problems. Indeed it sheds light on virtually every aspect of the Church's life and work. As a field of disciplined Christian study and research, it is of course a newcomer. In the days when the nations of Europe were regarded as almost totally Christian, the European state churches naturally did not concern themselves with church growth. When large numbers of Europeans settled in North and South America, Australia, or South Africa, the civilized areas of these new nations were also regarded as almost totally Christian. It was assumed that the new nations would be entirely Christianized as soon as the remaining natives were pacified. Serious study of the problems of church growth began in this present century as Christians began to be aware that their position does not automatically commend itself to everyone; that there are other important and influential traditions of human civilization; and that the "Christian nations" will not necessarily always hold the balance of world power.

In the first half of this century, thinking about church growth among English-speaking Christians was stimulated by that remarkable prophet and controversialist, Roland Allen. Allen was a priest of the Church of England who went to China at the end of the last century. After serving as a missionary for several years, he returned because of ill health and served for a short period as vicar of an English parish. Allen was overwhelmed by the awareness that the vast missionary effort being carried on by all denominations in China rested on such precarious foundations that it might be overthrown at a moment's notice. He was equally overwhelmed by the shallowness of the Church's hold on the minds and hearts of nominally Christian Englishmen. He saw that there were the same problems both "at home" and in "overseas missionary areas." Needless to say, most of Allen's contemporaries laughed at his gloomy warnings. Today, of course, we can see that Allen overstated nothing. After resigning from his parish in 1907, Allen spent the remainder of his long life studying, traveling all over the world, and writing books and articles on the renewal and revitalization of the Church's missionary work. His last years were spent in retirement in Kenya, where he died in 1947.[1]

Roland Allen was a learned and widely read man. His great inspiration was the simple fact that in the time of the Apostles the Christian Church spread with great rapidity through the cities and towns of the Near East, although the Church had extremely limited facilities for organization, communication, or education. In the face of this Allen reached an equally simple but far reaching conclusion: people themselves, when they accept the Christian faith, actually are able to organize their local church and to pass on their faith to others. Ordinary people, without any special background or lengthy training, are able to choose their leaders, maintain their discipline, and discover various practical means for implementing their beliefs. In secular life, people make similar decisions all the time, and they do so with passable success. If the Church will only accept its own teaching that its people are the children of God, members of Christ, and heirs of heaven, then the Church can move forward, as God may guide it, at every level and on every front.

Modern sociology provides impressive endorsement to Allen's self-taught social insights. All communities do in fact have leaders within them. Uneducated, isolated, and impoverished communities often have particularly skillful leaders, because the problems of survival for such communities are often so great. When awakened to a sense of selfhood and identity, even backward communities can give birth to strong constructive forces. Modern theology reminds us that Holy Baptism, as a sacrament of our incorporation into the full and perfect human personhood of Jesus Christ, should confer just such an awakening to selfhood and identity. Every baptized person shares in the royal priesthood of Jesus Christ. In the Church and in the world, every Christian is called to exercise the responsibilities and privileges of this lofty status.

During Allen's own lifetime, if his books were not always believed, they were at least widely circulated. Most of his major writings have been republished during the past few years.[2] His friends in England also founded the Survey Application Trust and the World Dominion Press, both of which have continued to concern themselves with church growth and related problems on an ecumenical and international scale. So much then at this point for Roland Allen. We will meet him again later.

In more recent years, the study of church growth has been energetically promoted by Dr. Donald A. McGavran, whose work as a missionary (Disciples of Christ), writer, and theological educator has long revolved around this concern, and whose books have popularized the expression "church growth" as a technical term.[3]

The Methodist Bishop, J. W. Pickett, made a significant contribution to thought in this field by his classic study of mass movements in India.[4] There have been a number of other persons, in various churches, who have carried out surveys and local studies that have shed light on this field. So far this work has been largely directed toward "foreign missions," that is to say, the extension of Western churches into Asia, Africa, Latin America, and the South Sea Islands, or into special groups with a "foreign" culture, such as certain Indian peoples, within the United States. A methodical analysis of missionary methods within the typical American city, town, or countryside is rarely made. Obviously the conclusions reached by studying church growth in other parts of the world, or within other cultures, will not all apply in the same way to the characteristic American scene. Yet certain basic principles regarding church growth have emerged, and these in fact are highly relevant to the situation in which many American churches find themselves. These principles are the primary object of our concern in the pages that follow.

Some Principles of Church Growth

First of all, church growth is not simply the accession of numbers as a result of human promotion. The Church belongs to God, and its growth is a gift from God. The Holy Spirit alone can initiate it. It is only in obedience to its Lord that the Church has a right to seek, receive, or retain its members.

The New Testament tells us a great deal about God's will for his Church. It is to be the New Israel, the People of God, God's Family, the Body of Christ, a spiritual Temple. Christianity is not embodied in a mere set of ideas or ethical principles. It is a living, visible community of people who hear the gospel, who are united to Christ by baptism and the gift of the Spirit, who pray in Christ's name, who partake of his body and blood, who care for the poor, and who love one another. God's first people, the Old Israel, was an exclusive community, limited to a particular ethnic group. The New Israel, the Church, is open to men and women of every nation, kindred, people, and tongue. The very nature of Christianity commits us to a concern for extending the Church. The nature of Christianity commits us to the belief that God wishes his Church to grow.

If growth is God's gift, the first and most basic thing we can do to obtain it is to pray to him for it. Our Lord taught us that our prayer must be insistent and persistent. Yet our historic liturgies were for the most part composed in an era when the Church was not concerned with missionary action. The usual traditional round of daily and weekly prayer does not force this topic on our attention. We must make a conscious and deliberate effort to pray for the extension and enlargement of the Church, and clergy and people need to be regularly reminded of this. What prayer should we regularly say for church growth? Perhaps the Lord's Prayer is not without relevance.

The Church must pray, but it must also watch. Having prayed, and put the matter into God's hands, we must accept what answer he gives, and in the way he gives it. God has a long-standing reputation for acting in inappropriate ways. A successful parish in a residential suburb may labor under the impression that everyone in the neighborhood belongs to some church. After praying for church growth, their eyes may suddenly be opened to a little pocket of unchurched immigrants who have been living for years on several inconspicuous little streets on the other side of the turnpike embankment. . . . A city church may be half empty because few Gentiles now live in the surrounding blocks of apartments. After putting the matter into God's hands, they may discover that many of those who are not Gentiles are no longer Jewish either, but that they hesitate to make themselves known to the church because of certain things which they have seen Christians do and heard Christians say. . . . A little country church may claim it cannot grow because there are not enough people in the area—only to learn that it is really the inability of the church to maintain a consistent schedule of services each week which has discouraged every newcomer for the past several years. . . . A large church may discover that growth forces it to found a daughter congregation with, as an immediate consequence, a temporary loss of parishioners to the mother parish. Precisely because it is God's gift, authentic church growth will often humble us, surprise us, and put us under judgment.

When new membership appears, it must be welcomed, nurtured, and cultivated. We receive new members for the glorification of God, not for the aggrandizement of our own prestige. This, too, must be said aloud. If we shut the door in the face of the converts God sends, he may not send any others. Obstacles must be removed. This is not to say that membership in the church should be made too easy, or that Christianity should be presented as a painless way of life. But misunderstandings, false emphases, and other barriers to communication must not be allowed to block the paths of those who are seeking the faith. Experience would appear to indicate that clergy and church officials can do little to precipitate church growth, but that they can very easily halt it. Above all, clergy and leading members of a congregation must never allow their own tastes and preferences to appear as standards to which new members must conform.

Ask an old and faithful member of any parish, large or small, in any part of the country, and he will almost invariably assure you that his parish is extremely friendly. He may even tell you that it is almost like a family. And indeed it is to him. As an old parishioner, he has known many members of the congregation for many years. Several are probably his neighbors, professional associates, or golf friends. Some may be relatives and descendants. In very small congregations where there has been little church growth for many years, it is not unusual to find that a large percentage of the people are tied to each other by blood or marriage. Naturally the church is like a family to them—it *is* their family.

The point is this: precisely the friendliness and family feeling of those inside the parish appear as aloofness and exclusiveness to those outside the parish. Look at such a parish through the eyes of a newcomer or inquirer. Everyone else knows each other by their first names, but he doesn't even know their last names. Everyone else knows each other's children, but perhaps the newcomer has no children, or if he has they too are strangers. After the service a group of people stand beside the road talking about some business, sports, or social gathering at which the newcomer had not been present. It is totally impossible for a stranger to feel anything except utterly ill-at-ease in this kind of friendly atmosphere. It is not surprising that the only newcomers who come, and continue to come, to a typical American church today are people who either already have, or immediately discover, some personal, professional, recreational, or cultural link with one or more members of the congregation, or who have children who are acceptable to the Sunday school, or who (in the case of younger people) are sufficiently like everyone else in appearance, speech, and manner to merit immediate social invitations.

This may sound like a terrible judgment on our parishes. In a negative sense it may be. But in a positive sense this tells us that the web of associations, relationships, and connections with which most of our lives are enmeshed provides the wires by which, in the providence of God, a vital contact with the Church may be begun. The minority of lonely people, who are not surrounded by family, professional, or recreational associations, would usually welcome the creation of such links. In short, it is the extremely miscellaneous and varied pattern of relationships with people in the secular world which offers the stepping stones on which the newcomer can enter.

The study of church growth indicates that people often join churches for reasons which seem inadequate, disappointing, or even quite unacceptable to well-trained and well-informed believers. If a pastor has worked hard to deliver intelligent sermons, to circulate good religious books, and to schedule well-planned courses of adult education, it is naturally disheartening to learn that a well-educated and mature couple has been attracted to his church (rather than some other) because they like the sound of the bells better, or because their son likes to play basketball in the parish house, or because the father admires the business acumen of one of the older members. Such reasons would indeed be outrageous for people who had the pastor's background and theological training. *But the newcomers have not had this background or training.* To people who have never experienced the reality of Christian faith and practice, superficial reasons may be the only reasons which could be meaningful at this point in their lives. God can use small and trivial things. People who are attracted by poor reasons may later be nurtured and challenged by better things. The woman who loves the bells may prove to be a sensitive musician who later makes an exceptional contribution to the life of the parish. The boy who likes basketball may later, by his fair play and fine sportsmanship, become a respected witness to the Christian faith in his college class. The serious businessman may later give many valuable hours of his time to unraveling the finances of a badly administered church hospital.

A corollary of this is the fact that the best evangelists may be the newcomers themselves. Those who have just joined a church know why they joined, and they can state their reasons to others who share their own background and hold the same values. Those who have just joined, furthermore, are still fully and actively in touch with those outside. A convert will often be asked by his friends and relatives why he took this step, and he will have the opportunity to tell them. After he has belonged a while, on the other hand, his friends and relatives who are not church people will lose interest, and will "agree to differ" with him on religious matters. As he becomes more fully assimilated to his church, he himself will probably prefer to talk about religion with those who share his faith, and so his channels of evangelistic communication gradually wither away.

The woman who loved the bells will learn that Christian doctrine attaches little value to them, and she will become too self-conscious and embarrassed to ask her musician friends to come simply to enjoy them. The basketball player, when he is instructed for confirmation, will be solemnly informed that athletic interest is no proper basis for Christian faith. (He may also be told not to invite friends

to play in the church's gym during unauthorized hours.)
The businessman father may discover that the old member
whom he had admired opposes many constructive steps in
the parish. And so their naïve enthusiasm for the church is
replaced by a faith erected on better foundations. To some
extent, this is as it should be. Meanwhile, however, this
family will have lost the desire and capacity to attract un-
evangelized and less informed friends to follow them over
the path they took.

In religious circles it is commonly assumed that only the
experienced and well-trained layman should be encouraged,
or even permitted, to be an active evangelist. Only the layman of long standing, who has acquired a very orthodox outlook, and who presents the Church in terms which the Church
itself favors, is really trusted. The study of church growth
indicates that this is a very dubious approach. It is precisely
those who are young in the faith, who have not assimilated
the characteristic attitudes and outlooks of the church member, who are best able to present Christianity in meaningful
terms to their peers. If the Church wishes to grow, it must
believe its own message enough to trust its people. Lay
action in the past has been thought of as activity by a few
chosen laymen working under clerical supervision. Effective
evangelism is not likely to take place on those terms. (In any
case, who wishes to join a church in which everything has
to be done under supervision?)

Lay action must be something which a large number of
laymen do in the way in which they themselves discover
they can do it best. It remains as the sacred responsibility
of the pastor to stimulate them at the outset, to encourage
them in the continuation, and at the end to show them that
their action has value only insofar as both their successes and
their failures can be offered up to God, through Jesus Christ,
in the fellowship of His life-giving Spirit.

But ye are a chosen generation, a royal priesthood, an holy nation, a special people; that ye should shew forth the praises of him who hath called you out of darkness into his marvellous light.

I Peter 2:9

These words were not addressed merely to ordained clergy, but to ordinary baptized men and women living in the world of their day.

2

DIMENSIONS OF MISSION

So far we have been considering church growth mainly in terms of individuals or families joining a congregation. It is easy to think in these terms, for any congregation is happy to welcome a new individual or a new family. A whole group of new people, however, who wish to have additional services to meet their convenience, or extra classes in Sunday school to accommodate their children, may not be so welcome. When a body of people representing another sociological or ethnic group appears, they may be received with suspicion. Likewise the formation of new congregations within an area may be opposed by existing congregations.

Individual accessions give the impression of growth and vitality, but without creating any strain on the structure of religious organizations. Yet ultimately, to think in individual terms is impossible. If new individuals keep coming into the Church, and if the older members are remaining faithful, the sum total must become larger and larger. Indeed, the mere fidelity of existing members must lead to substantial increases over the years as children are born and raised in the Church. Either small congregations will become larger, or else they will have to divide into new congregations, and as members move into new communities other new congregations must be initiated too. There is, furthermore, no foreseeable end to this process. The world's population continues to grow, and in recent decades, the non-Christian portion of the world's population has gained a gigantic majority over the Christian minority. This information may not make us feel comfortable but it is true, nonetheless. Even within the Christian portion of the United States, moreover, most people are far behind in their awareness of the sheer numbers which confront us.

The Spanish philosopher Ortega y Gasset has written of the burgeoning of peoples as the distinctive phenomenon of our time, inevitably influencing every aspect of life.

This fact is quite simple to enunciate, though not so to analyze. I shall call it the fact of agglomeration, of "plenitude." Towns are full of people, houses full of tenants, hotels full of guests, trains full of travellers, cafes full of customers, parks full of promenaders, consulting-rooms of famous doctors full of patients, theatres full of spectators, and beaches full of bathers.[1]

If this was true in 1930, when these words were first written, how much more so today, a generation and a half later!

The Christian churches of America have generally lagged so far behind the growth of peoples and the expansion of national life, that large numbers of nominal Christians assume that the churches are content to minister to a mere minority of the Christian population. The very fact that we have so many nominal Christians indicates the extent of the problem. To the New Testament, this very concept of nominal Christianity is unknown. To be baptized is to be brought into the Church, the visible community of Christian people. It is only as members of this community that we can have the full knowledge and authentic experience of what Christianity is. In short, by failing to commit itself to maintaining a sufficient community to contain all its baptized people, the Church (or a church) compromises its own position. As long as the effective scope of an ecclesiastical body is so small that a large proportion of its members are constantly lapsing into a nominal status, that body can no longer claim that its message is urgent, or that its disciplines are binding, or that its ministrations are necessary. The study of church growth involves the Church's integrity.

There is no doubt that many good and loyal church people, and many leading officials, feel an opposition to church growth on intuitive and emotional grounds. Many American families like to feel that their roots lie in a small town or rural area. The remembered or imagined picture of the small-town church, with its kindly pastor, its neighborly parishioners, and its well-behaved children, plays an important role in American ideology. Today, if we are jostled about by crowds of people all week, as many of us are, we wish, at least on Sundays, to have the reassurance of worshiping with a smaller, more personal group. We do not wish our parish to succumb to the pressure for expansion. And so we do not welcome talk of church growth.

I would say that every link in this chain has some plausibility except the final conclusion. Many of us in fact do come from small towns. Many of us did receive our early spiritual nurture in the context of a small parish. Many of us still prefer to worship in small churches and to have our children reared within them. All of that is well and good. *But it is no argument against church growth.* If small churches are preferable, and possibly they are, then let us found many more. It is evident that the existing number of small churches will not be sufficient to serve our children and grandchildren. Furthermore, unless the problems of church growth are faced, large numbers of small churches will continue to go out of existence every year. The vitality of the best old-fashioned small parishes will not be recovered or preserved in a context of stagnation or decline.

This can readily be observed in many of the rural communities in which our grandparents or great-grandparents lived. All across the country, we see little village churches of many denominations which have closed. The membership became so small that the church could no longer operate. Some denominations have virtually withdrawn from whole regions. Often congregations are merged, but this frequently does no good. You can't pull a wagon with a team of dying horses. No amount of jurisdictional or interdenominational cooperation can help a church which is unable to hold or attract new members to replace those who die or move away. Such churches may, at one time, have met the problems of church growth very adequately, but if they cannot meet these problems today and tomorrow, they will cease to exist. The little church, which is a valued part of the American Christian heritage, cannot continue unless the responsible governing bodies face the question of church growth.

On the other hand, let not the larger parishes suppose that this is no concern of theirs. American cities are littered with the vast Gothic carcasses of churches of every denomination which supposed that they had solved the question of church growth. The sociological and economic factors which bring people into an area in one decade will take them out in another. In a fluid society, every parish must be constantly seeking new members or it will soon be ministering to a nonresident congregation, with an increasing percentage of lapses. Any parish which expects its people to be faithful for their entire lives must expect that a large percentage of them will join new parishes, and in many cases these will have to be newly founded parishes in growing areas. If this expectation is not clearly articulated, and if there are not sufficient new parishes to receive the mobile new generation in new neighborhoods, then individuals, families, and entire neighborhoods will come to assume that a nominal allegiance is all that their church really expects of them. From a literal and pragmatic point of view, they will be all too correct.

Corollaries of Growth

Today, many aspects of life have been dissociated from Christian values. Philosophers and historians tell us that we have entered a post-Christian era. Yet God continues to call people into the Christian Church. In communities that are described as overchurched, some congregations continue to grow. In communities which are irreligious in their whole spirit and atmosphere, some congregations continue to grow. In communities where other churches have closed their doors and moved away, some congregations continue to grow. In communities where the total population and economy are declining, some congregations continue to grow.

Growing churches may be large or small. They may be rich or poor. They may represent privileged or handicapped portions of the population. They may be individual congregations, or they may be groups of congregations growing throughout an area, and the area of growth may itself be large or small. In any case, a growing church, precisely because it is growing, can exercise its influence and implement its faith in ways which a static or declining church cannot. Several illustrations may clarify this important point.

Most ecclesiastical bodies have serious concerns for education. Yet it is difficult for a static or shrinking church to do anything in this field. Such a church ultimately consists mostly of older people, whose period of learning is past. They may be very well-informed, knowledgeable folk, but they are inevitably defensive about their declining church and accordingly resist new religious ideas. A growing church, on the contrary, has new members who look forward to new training both for themselves and for their children. Their religious views are more oriented toward the future, and so the educative process can operate.

Since a growing church normally has a higher proportion of younger people, it can have an effective program in schools and colleges. A static or shrinking church may inaugurate ambitious projects, but without the constituency of students such projects are unlikely to succeed.

In the field of social relations, church growth is also an important factor. Any religious body may witness to Christian principles by issuing public statements decrying injustice. Such statements may be necessary, but when do they contribute most to the improvement of the situation? The nature of democratic government is such that any very large religious body can gain a hearing from public officials. Smaller bodies are less likely to, and they certainly will have little influence on practical politics if they are declining in numbers. A growing religious movement can readily make itself heard, particularly if it is growing within an area of dispute and unrest. We cannot talk realistically about social witness while ignoring the fact that in a democratic society numbers count. It is people, not empty buildings, that will mold the future, and the churches which are people's churches can make Christian influence effectively felt.

Church growth is also significant for ecumenical relations. The union of declining religious groups is hardly an object that can command enthusiasm. Members of such churches are naturally defensive and look backward. Growing religious bodies, on the other hand, look forward. They can assimilate new elements and adapt to new situations. Precisely because they are growing, they provide an increasing number of new positions for new leadership. This is the kind of context within which we would all wish ecumenical developments to take place. A growing religious movement is extending its influence over more and more people, and as it casts a larger shadow on the future it can make stronger claims on the present commitment of its followers.

The Corporate Foundations of Church Growth

As has been said, church growth cannot long be thought of simply in terms of individuals. Congregations, and groups of congregations, ultimately must be considered. It is in terms of these larger groupings, furthermore, that Christian teaching regarding society as a whole can be expressed and implemented. The study of this field indicates that the process of conversion and enrollment in a religious body is far more of a corporate act than has been commonly recognized in our society.

Three points of considerable importance emerge. (1) The qualitative value of the individual conversion is not always so great as has sometimes been assumed. (2) Undue reliance on individual accessions tends to limit a church to those cultural and sociological groups in which the individual has freedom of movement. (3) Even in those cultural and sociological horizons within which individuals are highly independent, significant religious commitment usually rests on underlying corporate factors. Each of these three points deserves some comment and we may take them up in order.

First, there is the quality and depth of individual religious decisions. For several centuries, Western civilization has prided itself on the freedom of individual persons to make free and reasonable decisions. Descartes's conception of the intellect as moving freely within a world of abstract rational truths is a classic philosophic formulation of this outlook. In religious circles, a person who joins a church in defiance of his family and associates is often admired for his sincerity and earnestness. Conversely, a person who simply follows his friends and relatives into a religious body is viewed as lacking in spiritual depth. McGavran's studies have demonstrated, in a most interesting manner, that such evaluations are apt to be very misleading. His testimony, coming as it does from one whose background is classic American "Free Church" Protestantism, is certainly impressive.[2] Isolated individual converts. like everyone else, are effected by mixtures of motive. Desire to rebel against one's family background and training is often a factor. Some people choose to belong to a church which their friends and associates do not belong to precisely because they do not wish to accept the corporate and social obligations of normal church life. Individual decisions are not always good decisions, or genuinely free decisions.

Second, because emphasis on the independent individual has been part of modern Western civilization, this emphasis is valued by those who are conscious heirs of this background. On the other hand, the overwhelming majority of human beings live in cultures and civilizations which do not recognize individual independence as desirable or constructive. In such cultures, dutiful, conscientious, and spiritually sensitive people are not inclined to make important individual decisions. If Christianity is to be effective in the international world of today, this has to be recognized. Even within our own society, furthermore, members of many particular groups find it virtually impossible to make independent commitments. To force the individual to do so will only be to tear him out of his background and impair his social effectiveness.[3] In such cases, to receive a group of individuals or families into a church more or less together may be much more desirable, even though some members of the group are less enthusiastic or less well prepared than others. Deaf persons, for instance, usually find it important to belong to a church to which a number of other deaf persons belong. Theological considerations are apt to take a secondary place, and this may as well be recognized. Yet work with the deaf is highly important if the work of the Christian Church is to have any visible resemblance to the work of Jesus Christ as recorded in the Gospels. For slightly different reasons, effective work with the culturally handicapped also involves the necessity of dealing with cohesive groups, the individual members of which may not be able to give a clear or rational explanation of their beliefs. In short, a church which is limited to free, independent individuals will gradually find itself largely limited to an upper-middle-class professional group —and this group is ultimately just as much a prey to its own shortcomings as any other!

This brings us to the third point. Even in a free individualistic society, important decisions are in fact rarely made in isolation. The people we live with, work with, and share our leisure time with, all influence us in a thousand ways. More subtly, we are also molded by the tastes and convictions of those with whom we would like to live, work, or play. When certain channels of association happen to bring people through the doors of the faith, it is important to keep these channels clear and the doors open. For the particular group of people involved, this may be the only time that their lives will head this way. As more members of a group are drawn into a church, the attraction for the remaining members of the same group becomes stronger and stronger. It is not here being proposed that we should simply use social pressure to manipulate people into the Church willy-nilly. Rather, it is being pointed out that social pressures are, in fact, shaping people's lives all of the time—whether the people know it or not. The Church can act more wisely and more responsibly if this fact is recognized. The individual within any sociological group can make a more authentic, more meaningful —and ultimately more free—decision to accept the Christian faith if it is presented in terms of the language, values, and feelings of his own group, somewhat superficial though these may sometimes be.

In speaking of the freedom of the individual to accept or reject the gospel, Paul Tillich has said:

There is always a genuine decision against the Gospel for those for whom it is a stumbling block. But this decision should not be dependent on the wrong stumbling block, namely, the wrong way of our communication of the Gospel—our inability to communicate. What we have to do is to overcome the wrong stumbling block in order to bring people face to face with the right stumbling block and enable them to make a genuine decision.[4]

As has been said, the newcomer who comes to a church and continues to come is held by a web of diverse human associations, ties, and interests. Later on, as a more experienced and more trained church member, he will acquire deeper and stronger roots, but these latter cannot be expected in the newly converted. If a parish church, like St. Peter, is successfully to fish for men, it must be ready to drop its net boldly and be prepared for a large catch. If the church is unable to manage a netful, it may find that it cannot attract isolated individuals either. In the next chapter we will consider how churches can actually expand their structure so that new growth, new work, and new responsibilities can be faced constructively.

3

EXTENDING
THE ORDAINED MINISTRY

If the Church is to grow, if the Church is to adapt itself to new opportunities, if the Church is to be young again, then it must be flexible. Its structure must be capable of extension. Subjected to change, or even to strong vibrations, a rigid structure cracks and breaks, but a flexible and living structure stretches. Stretching is also the gesture of those who are waking up.

If the Church is to face the future, it must be outwardly and visibly a body that is flexible, limber, and growing. This must be demonstrated and seen on the corporate and official level. Everyone knows that Churches can be flexible—perhaps too flexible—in their treatment of individuals and families. And every church member knows that individual clergymen can be flexible in regard to their own work. Indeed in many cases the amount and variety of work laid upon them have been already long ago stretched far beyond what any reasonable and responsible employer would expect or permit. Yet the corporate and official structure within which the clergy stand remains peculiarly rigid in nearly every major Christian body. The organizational framework of which they are officers usually shows little new life. And the prevailing methods for selecting, training, assigning, supervising, and pensioning clergy usually indicate little awareness of the changes that are taking place both in the Christian Church and in the modern world.

Let us now consider some of the ways in which the structural rigidity of the ministerial system strangles vitality and growth at the local level, and let us then go on to see how extendability and expandability can be introduced. In discussing this topic, however, there are problems. It is simple enough to engage in optimistic generalizations about missionary outreach, but when one actually faces the question of how to reach out and how to develop a pattern that reaches out, then one also faces the fact that different situations require somewhat different answers to such questions. Different denominations have differing arrangements and organizational structures, and some structures, even within the same religious body, differ in various geographical areas. It is extremely interesting, nonetheless, to see the similarities. If one wishes to understand "the spontaneous expansion of the Church and the causes which hinder it," [1] then one must train one's eye to discern certain recurring patterns, and to recognize them even when camouflaged by the externals of a tradition different from one's own.

Different Christian churches have different emphases and different theological interpretations of their ordained ministries. Yet most American Christians, at least within the prevailing middle-class sector, tend to assimilate the clergyman to a single level. Some view him as above all a preacher, others of us emphasize his priestly and sacramental responsibilities, yet all have tended to see him "graded off" at approximately the same social, legal, and professional level.

From the point of view of church growth, this professional stereotyping of the Christian ministry is intolerable, and informed clergy and laity should reject it with the utmost vigor. The New Testament insists that within the Body of Christ different members have different functions, and Christian history confirms the importance of this teaching. The present chapter will indicate several types of situations within which a diversification of ministerial roles and office can in fact open the door to church growth.

The Small Church in a Difficult Area

The visible inability of a church to extend itself has definite effects on the concrete local situation. We may first consider areas where there are small and relatively static congregations, as in thinly populated rural regions, or in certain old bypassed residential areas of cities, or within small minority groups. In such situations, the congregation is often made up of some intensely loyal older people, together with a few children or younger people. Such a congregation is regularly depleted by the fact that young adults who grew up in the church marry persons of another background, or of no religious background at all, and then do not bring up their own children in the church. Why, clergy ask, do loyal old members allow their children or grandchildren to lapse? The study of church growth indicates the answer. Older people are loyal because they remember the church as it was fifty years ago, and because their peers, of their own age and background, are still active members of it. But because the church has given no visible evidence of ability to keep pace, even with the numerical growth of the church's own families, these people do not seriously expect all their children to remain in it. Their children and grandchildren are not, after all, part of the fifty-year-old picture they treasure.

Such a congregation does not offer enough money, or enough work, to retain the full-time service of a resident clergyman. Hence it has frequently shared a pastor with one or two other neighboring places. Often he will be a newly ordained man fresh from seminary who has been assigned to such a charge. He will generally remain a year or so, and there will be an interval before his successor arrives. In some cases, such men will find this experience embittering and frustrating, and they will carry into their later ministry a tacit hostility and suspicion toward small missions. In other cases, they will secure a gratifying response in the community and will be much missed when they leave the little church. People in these small congregations learned years ago that a less competent man is preferable to a more competent one, because the better man will be called away sooner to a larger and "more important" position. In such a context, growth, vitality, or progress of any sort becomes virtually unattainable. To blame the people themselves for the stagnation of their congregation is absurd, for the system imposed on them makes anything except stagnation impossible.

Since the static small church is perennially dependent on financial aid from more prosperous congregations elsewhere, its people develop little stewardship or real sense of responsibility for their church. Since regional offices of the church inevitably regret this perennial drain on their resources, the little mission is resented, and its people sometimes know this. They cannot be enthusiastic, or actively promote their religion, if they are aware of constant efforts to have their chapel closed. Since some of these people know the Church only in terms of their own congregation, they have no other frame of reference or basis of loyalty. Since most regions have a number of these small static congregations, much of the budget for domestic missions each year is swallowed up in this static work, and hence new and more promising projects cannot be undertaken. So the contagion of frustration and discouragement spreads. One could hardly imagine a clearer example of the inability of a rigid clerical system to adapt itself to the actual needs of people. This may seem to some people a rather exaggerated, gloomy picture. Yet precisely such situations exist in every state of America, and in many other parts of the world.

What is the answer to these problematical little congregations? There is no answer which can guarantee a transition from stagnation to new life, but there is an answer which at least opens the door to new life, which can at least make new vitality a possibility. This answer is quite simply to relieve static churches of the burden of an inappropriate and unworkable system in regard to the ordained ministry. Instead of an intermittent succession of temporary clergy, the people in most of these places should simply be asked to choose their own pastor from among the experienced and respected older men of their own congregation (or, in some cases, from a group of adjacent congregations).

In most cases, the choice will be an obvious one. As Roland Allen pointed out long ago, every religious group must have some leadership within it, or else it could not exist. In many cases, the recognized and inevitable leader will be the layman who has kept the church going during the numerous intervals between clergy. Obvious though the leader may be, however, the congregation should have a real choice in calling him to the sacred ministry. In many little missions and chapels, this will be the first serious decision which the Church authorities have ever allowed the local congregation to make, even though these same people are quite accustomed to making serious choices in other aspects of life. Having been chosen by his peers, furthermore, the designated man will have a kind of leadership and local authority which no one sent in from outside the community would be likely to acquire.

Such a man should then be prepared for ordination in the simplest and most rapid manner that the rules of the church permit. As Allen has pointed out, St. Paul could have local leaders ready for ordination in a year or less.[2] Today we demand more training but we can do the job with much improved facilities for rapid adult education. Undue delay can only create frustration and suspicion. Excessive training, furthermore, will only destroy such a man's ability to express his faith in the thought patterns of his own community. Attendance at a seminary, exposure to academic traditions and affectations, and the orientation toward Europe characteristic of higher theological study would undoubtedly ruin such a man—just as it has and does ruin so many others. When such a man, chosen and trained in his own local community, is finally ordained, the relation of the static little congregation to the Church at large will be suddenly and drastically changed. For the first time, the Church will be taking the small congregation seriously. Its people will be recognized as full-fledged, responsible human beings. For the first time, a Christian relationship will exist between the larger Church and the little mission. It may not always be an easy or a happy relationship, but it will be a Christian one, and where Christian relationships exist the Holy Spirit is free to operate.

Needless to say, such a man must remain in his secular job or occupation until retirement. This will not only provide him with his livelihood, but will also safeguard his own sense of identity and his authentic role in the local community. Since the payment of a clergyman is normally the principal operating expense of a small congregation, with the ordination of a self-supporting leader, economic dependence on outside resources can cease. Thereafter, the congregation can consider in terms of its own needs and capacities the maintainance of its building, the support of its program, and some contribution to the work of the Church elsewhere. In many cases, this would revolutionize planning and strategy. With the bulk of missionary funds no longer committed to static or declining congregations, significant support could be given to experimental and forward-looking projects. Existing hostility toward domestic missions could be overcome. Young seminary graduates, furthermore, would not have to begin their ministries in an atmosphere of bitterness and frustration, but could instead be assigned to work in growing parishes, under mature and experienced clergy who could give them the supervision they need.

Many conservative American Christians, accustomed to the

stereotyped pattern of the ordained ministry as a professionally trained middle-class occupation, may be startled at the
proposal to ordain men of limited education who, after ordination, may continue to engage in some other occupation or
profession. But is such a proposal as radical as it seems? Our
Lord was a carpenter, and his first Apostles were professional
fishermen. When the Christian Church finally acquired an
educated theologian in the person of St. Paul, he nonetheless
chose to earn his living in a secular occupation and found that
it facilitated his missionary work to do so.[3] During the early
centuries of Christian history, many Christian clergy sup-
ported themselves partially or entirely by secular occupations.[4] In agricultural parts of Europe, village parsons have
continued down into modern times to farm the plots of land
with which the local church was frequently endowed. In
Greek villages, when a new priest is needed, the local people
still literally elect a devout and respected citizen of the village
and present him to the bishop for ordination.[5] Such a system
has remained workable in spite of centuries of poverty and
oppression, and as Turks, Nazis, and Communists have discovered to their chagrin, this kind of Christianity can inspire
the deepest loyalty and courage.

Within the history of America, we see many religious
movements which have had great vigor while they were willing to make full use of capacities for leadership whenever
they appeared. The early Methodists were by no means the
only example. Certainly the massive alignment of American
Negroes with the Baptist tradition is a testimony to the willingness of Baptists to allow new congregations to form and to
choose their pastor without being encumbered with impossible economic and administrative commitments. The continued rapid growth of new Baptist congregations in many
areas illustrates the same principle. One may respect this
principle regardless of how one feels about certain other aspects of Baptist faith or practice.

Roland Allen maintained that the freeing of the ordained

ministry from a professional straitjacket was the crucial question of missionary strategy for the twentieth century. There can be no doubt that when it has been so freed, results have followed. In a survey of non-Roman churches in South America, the English missionary theologian Douglas Webster has gathered very interesting data.[6] Almost all the rapidly growing denominations make extensive use of clergy who earn their livings in other professions. South American Pentecostals, one of the most rapidly growing Christian movements anywhere in the world, rely almost exclusively on self-supporting ministers trained through a system of apprenticeship. In much the same vein, the American authority Eugene A. Nida has written of the type of training for such a ministry which characteristically appears among the "indigenous Churches" showing strong and rapid growth at the local level:

. . . training for leadership in the indigenous Churches follows an apprenticeship system. . . . by the informal structuring of training through a series of increasingly important responsibilities, potential leaders are both prepared for their work and constantly screened by the test of practical accomplishment. As a result, the leaders of such indigenous movements are often highly competent.[7]

Another dramatic example is provided by the worker-priest movement in France from 1944–1954.[8] Here we find a number of well-trained, highly dedicated professional middle-class clergy deliberately entering the milieu of the working man. They discovered not only great opportunities for the exercise of their ministries, but also a spiritual enrichment which they themselves could receive. They discovered what the Church sometimes forgets, that the witnessing Christian is first and foremost called to be a man—with the dignity, responsibility, and full humanness which are proper to man. Whatever may be said of the worker-priest experience, it was not suppressed because it failed, but because its success was too great a threat to its powerful opponents. Christians of every denomination are encouraged to know that this heroic movement is again beginning to reassert itself here and there. Among European Protestants, a similar outlook is also manifested in the Community of Taizé. Many of the brothers have secular trades or professions which they continue to exercise. In the small ecumenical house which Taizé has established on the South Side of Chicago, their pattern has been continued, with several of the brothers working in jobs of various kinds in the surrounding city.

The present writer has elsewhere recorded many examples of clergy in various parts of the world who have lived and worked effectively within the economic and social structure of the community in which they found themselves.[9] They may be less educated, or more educated, than the typical middle-class professional clergyman. They may be richer or poorer. They may be more or less pious. The point is that they do provide a stable ministry of word and sacrament in communities where such a ministry does not otherwise exist. They do so, furthermore, without depriving the community of its self-respect and sense of responsibility—as the familiar system of continued external subsidization inevitably does.

It is in no sense being suggested here that the Church has no need of the theologically trained professional clergyman. Quite the contrary. We will need more such men, and better-trained men, than we are likely to get during the next few decades. Yet the professionally trained and professionally oriented clergyman does not diminish the need for other types of clergy, doing other types of work. Indeed the theologians and scholars, the experienced ecclesiastical administrators, and the skilled preachers, counselors, and teachers— all these will have their effectiveness radiated out into far wider circles if they can be surrounded by an echelon of less specialized, less institutionalized clergy who mediate and communicate the Church's message to the ordinary people on the less sophisticated level. The nonprofessional clergy-

man, the village pastor or worker-priest, will constantly look
to the highly trained specialist for resource and guidance.
What a godsend it would be for many a bored and frustrated
clergyman if he could share his training and his theological
knowledge with a group of responsible and responsive local
people who were putting this knowledge to work in concrete
ways! How many intelligent and intellectually aspiring young
men go through our best theological schools, and master vast
realms of Scripture, history, and doctrine, and then in subsequent years never have anyone with whom they can discuss
these things! Is it any wonder that when some of them are
middle-aged the only "theology" they can recall consists of
wornout clichés, and their "serious study" consists of reading
several superficial popular books about religion each year?
The opportunity to train a few local men for the ordained
ministry would provide for many of our professional and
highly educated clergy the first chance in their careers to
utilize fully their own education. The development of such
a nonprofessional ministry in the so-called "difficult areas"
would thus not only give a wider and more stable administration of word and sacrament to the laity, but it would also
bring new life, new stimulus, and new hope to many a man in
the ranks of the professional and theologically trained clergy.

Finally, let the reader recall that this is not an interesting
speculative question to be pondered about in a leisurely and
aloof manner. There are mountain towns a short drive from
New York, Washington, or Pittsburgh where desperately
poor, frustrated, and hopeless people look to snake-handlers,
faith-healers, and self-appointed prophets as the only spokes-
men for the good news of the gospel. The members of the
educated and more orthodox Christian bodies feel conde-
scending pity—but have our churches provided any viable
plan or strategy for planting responsible and self-respecting
parishes through these regions? There are Indian groups all
over Western America who would like to hear sermons, pray,

and receive the sacraments in their own tongue—yet no white clergyman serving in the area knows their language or is likely to learn it. And so we tell them that one of their own men can be ordained—after he has completed college and a suitable course in an accredited seminary. This is indeed helpful advice in a community where no one has more than a sixth-grade education! Or one can look at the dispossessed minorities inhabiting the polyglot ghettos of every large city. Conservative Americans sometimes wonder why the depressed classes have not been more deeply touched by Christianity. But they have been touched. They have accepted the message that God loves them and cares about them. They have accepted the Christian call to self-respect and self-determination. For this reason people of these shabby back streets do not wish to be second-class members of the big, half-empty, brownstone churches of Main Street. For this reason they do not wish to be third-class members of the respectable denominations which will not let them have parishes of their own, or allow their own people to be ordained on conditions which they could fulfill. These are not questions to be answered ten or twenty years from now. These questions have screamed for a solution for many decades. Many of these peoples have already given up all hope in the Church. Many more give up every year. Is the Church simply an old institution that can give old answers to old questions, or has it enough vitality, enough flexibility, enough youth, to act today to meet immediate needs? The "small church in a difficult area" is indeed on a crucial firing line in a major battle.

The Modest or Medium-Sized Congregation

As we move from the small to the somewhat larger congregation, in an ordinary American community, church growth usually appears in a different form, but again it is frequently curtailed by the Church's structure. One often sees a moderate-sized parish which is described as having "grown slightly," or as having "having held its own," during the past fifteen or twenty years. If the population of the surrounding neighborhood has doubled or quadrupled during this same period, then in fact the church has not held its own. In relation to the community as a whole, it has declined at a very rapid rate. This is a common example of strangled church growth. When the parish declines, the people who remain most enthusiastic about it may often be declining people, who have lost their own effective relationship to the community and who accordingly welcome the haven which a restricted church provides. Here we see the urgent pastoral and spiritual importance of church growth. Church growth is needed, not to drive these declining people out, but to restore to them their own identity as effective, creative persons within an effective and creative Christian body.

The first flush of church growth in a modest congregation usually leads to an expansion and renovation of the physical plant, which is invariably more expensive than anticipated. In an area that is not affluent, this means that finances thereafter become critical. The clergyman is characteristically overworked, and the parish cannot afford to hire him an assistant. Any further growth will accordingly mean thinner and less adequate pastoral care. Honest facing of this should, in the first instance, lead to the assuming of a fuller role by lay people. They can exercise positive responsibilities in every aspect of the church's life. Lay readers can have a noticeable part in all the services of worship every Sunday throughout the year. Articulate lay people, rather than the clergyman, can arrange and lead adult programs of religious education. Some special group or guild can undertake calling on the sick and aged. Certain mature and experienced men and women may be able to handle some cases of pastoral counseling, and arrange referrals to welfare agencies when necessary. The parish can designate certain individuals to represent it on the local boards and civic committees which often cut heavily into the clergyman's time. As indicated in an earlier chapter, *inexperienced* lay people can be effective evangelists. And lay people can train other lay people to do these things. Let it be said again, there is no area or aspect of the church's life and work to which lay people cannot make some positive contribution. Most clergy are intellectually in favor of this, but unfortunately their usual training and background have not prepared them to work with lay people in this way. Patience, frankness, and determination are needed on the part of all concerned.

As lay people assume fuller responsibility, the entire life of the parish will be strengthened, and it will be able to minister effectively to a somewhat larger number of people. Sooner or later, nonetheless, the clergyman needs ordained assistance. Church growth is not, after all, the extension of a human organization. Nor is it merely the diffusion of Christian ideas and attitudes. The Church is a community founded on the Word of God and his life-giving sacraments. The ministry of word and sacrament must stand at the center of the Church's life. To be able to grow the Church must be able to demonstrate in visible fashion its ability to extend and enlarge this ministry when needed and as needed in local situations. How can this need be met in areas where funds to employ assistant clergy do not exist?

Here we may as well face the fact that the Christian Church has, from the earliest times, had a distinct order of assistant ministers. For the Church to plan its strategy and pursue its mission as if such an order did not exist is neither truthful nor helpful. This assisting office is the diaconate, or order of deacons. In the annals of Christian history the diaconate has had a glorious place. Yet in modern times its position, or even its existence, has hardly been known to many informed Christians. Today the ecumenical movement, liturgical reform, and Vatican Council II have all called for new attention to the diaconate.

lay leaders - deacons

In the early centuries, when the Church was a dynamic and rapidly growing movement, deacons exercised a great many functions everywhere, and the diaconate included such notable figures as St. Lawrence of Rome and St. Vincent of Spain. During the Middle Ages, however, when all Europe was Christianized, church life became increasingly standardized within a rigid framework. The conception of the ordained ministry was stratified, and the diaconate was reduced to a brief apprenticeship, through which a clergyman passed prior to being ordained as a priest. Only exceptional figures, like St. Francis, chose to remain as deacons throughout life. On the parish level, the order of deacons dropped out of sight throughout Western Europe. This has remained the situation within Roman Catholicism.[10] A young clergyman is ordained a deacon during his last year of seminary, but usually has little or no opportunity to exercise his ministry until he has been ordained a priest the next year. This arrangement has recently become an object of criticism. Within progressive circles, the proposal is now made that some married men be ordained to the diaconate as a lifelong vocation, and this proposal has received some support from the recent Vatican Council.[11]

The Orthodox Churches of Eastern Europe likewise treat the diaconate as a brief formal step on the way to the priesthood, yet they have also retained the older conception of the diaconate as a genuine vocation. Assistants to bishops are frequently clergy who serve as deacons for many years before entering the priesthood. Likewise, large parish churches may have a deacon who assists the priest on Sundays and feasts, but who engages in secular work on weekdays.[12]

In various other churches, deacons occupy varying roles. In Presbyterian and other Reformed Churches, deacons are traditionally lay officers responsible for the finances of the parish. In many cases, however, their role is not clearly differentiated from that of the lay elder.[13] In churches having the Independent or Congregational type of government, the board of deacons tends to be the lay governing body, the deacons apparently having displaced the elders from this function.[14] The pastoral needs of the present time, and current ecumenical discussions, all strongly indicate the desirability, in these churches, for a theoretical and practical clarification of the nature of these offices. Irrespective of what terminology be used, it is important that "the minister" be aided by assisting ministers, drawn from the local congregation, and possessing some recognized degree of responsibility. Terminology is not to be disregarded, however, and the demands of Christian unity reinforce the desirability of using accepted traditional terms with recognizable and customary meanings.

The Lutheran Churches inherited the deaconless parishes of medieval Western Europe, and the diaconate has not been visible in most of Lutheranism. In the last century, it was partially revived in Germany in the form of a lay association, or brotherhood, of Christian social service workers. Various proposals have been recently made for a more general diaconate in Lutheranism.[15]

The Episcopal Church has had a unique, if limited, experience. Like other churches of the Anglican Communion throughout the world, the Episcopal Church has inherited the medieval view of the diaconate as an apprenticeship. When he finishes his theological studies, an aspirant for the ministry is first ordained a deacon. After serving in this capacity, usually for a year, he is ordained a priest. In each century, only a very few men have served as deacons for extended periods, or for life.[16] Yet the canonical legislation of the Episcopal Church has long made some provision for men of less specialized background to enter the diaconate. At present the requirements are very flexible. The diaconate is quite explicitly recognized as a possible permanent vocation within the church for men who continue to support themselves by secular occupations.[17] At present, somewhat less than three hundred men are serving on this basis in America and most of them are exercising very constructive ministries, assisting within parishes in the administration of the sacraments,[18] visiting the sick, and conducting instructions, and doing other things according to their personal abilities and the differing needs of local situations. In some cases, these men have been serving in one or more parishes for many years with very fruitful results, and this can hardly now be called an experiment. Proof of effectiveness has long ago become objective fact. Yet the men now serving as permanent deacons, and those currently preparing for this office, are only a minute fraction of the thousands of experienced and reliable churchmen, in every part of the country and in every class of society, who could train for this assisting ministry if the church encouraged them to do so. It is regrettable that in many dioceses the academic requirements for ordination are so exaggerated that the very sort of man who should be a deacon is permanently debarred.[19] Early retirement from many businesses and occupations is presenting all American churches with a veritable army of men in good health, with a wide range of experience and human ability, many of whom are seeking some constructive field of activity, with little or no need for financial remuneration. It is to be hoped that ecclesiastical leadership will become sensitive to the extraordinary opportunities and responsibilities which this new situation presents. It is also to be hoped that the actual congregations will in the future have a greater share in summoning men to the diaconate. The rector of a well-known Episcopal parish in a recent statement reported thus:

Many of us are persuaded that the diaconate is not an "inferior" ministry at all, but that it has its own purpose and function which is meaningful to the parish and thus to the whole Church. Fortunate is that parish which has one or more permanent deacons.

Out of my own experience, having presented three men to my

bishop for ordination to the perpetual diaconate, I am persuaded that almost any parish can find at least one man who would prepare himself for this order and would gladly serve as an ordained deacon—not for money, but out of obedience to the call and the will of God and his Church.[20]

In conjunction with the diaconate, one goes on to think of the order of deaconesses. They too had a conspicuous role in ancient centuries, but later lapsed into oblivion and their duties were in some measure taken over by other kinds of religious sisterhoods. The order was revived among German Lutherans during the last century on a large and very successful scale.[21] To a lesser extent, many other churches have subsequently provided for such a vocation, and many outstanding dedicated women have served in this capacity. Today, the deaconesses face a certain crisis in many of the churches which have such an order. There has been the desire to safeguard the status of the order by confining its membership to a highly trained and extremely dedicated group of women who will live a life of great austerity and will not be handicapped by any family ties or obligations. As often happens when institutions are safeguarded, the effect of this policy is virtually to wipe out the institution being "safeguarded." Women who desire a highly disciplined life are likely to prefer the conventual sisterhoods, but those who wish an active ministry in the world of today are offended by the traditionalist outlook of the deaconesses. It is evident that if the order is to enjoy any new life during the remainder of this century, many of its customs and patterns must be modernized. Permission for some deaconesses to engage in secular jobs, and the possibility of some of them being married, are proposals which obviously arise. The consideration of these questions has been encouraged by the World Council of Churches and by Diakonia, the World Federation of Deaconess Associations, an international and ecumenical agency.[22]

Among the most creative modern efforts to provide a viable structure for an officially authorized ministry of women is that of the Church of South India.[23] Known either as the Order for Women, or as the Sisters of the Church, it was inaugurated in Bangalore on Whitsunday in 1952. Since then it has established an important place for itself in the Church of South India and it is closely linked with both the program and the leadership of the general women's organization of that church. Its members usually wear a white and blue sari and sandals (or go barefoot). Some of them live alone or in small groups in "ashrams" or retreat houses where they devote themselves to prayer, mediation, and the spiritual guidance of others. These may be said to follow an Indian adaptation of the conventual life of traditional sisterhoods and monastic orders for women. Others within the order devote themselves to teaching, evangelism, and social service work such as is usually associated with deaconesses.[24] Thus both active and contemplative vocations, and several stages in between, are comfortably accommodated within a single order which is linked with the total structure of the church in various ways. Such an arrangement has much to commend it.

Various churches also have other associations, orders, and agencies which are germane to our discussion. Voluntary lay organizations may offer very constructive help. Within Roman Catholicism, sisters of various orders perform outstanding work at the local level. The Eastern Orthodox and the Episcopal Churches also have communities of sisters, but in the United States they have been too few to have been frequently seen in the average parish. Among Lutheran and Reformed Churches, there has been strong historic opposition even to the existence of such a vocation, yet today Christians of many varieties are reconsidering many such questions. In Europe, small groups of Protestant sisters have emerged in recent years, and are winning widespread respect.[25] We may assume that some similar groups will appear in America in the years ahead. The question is whether or not they will receive the support and encouragement which they will deserve and need.

An interesting lay organization which we will encounter in the next chapter is the Church Army of the Episcopal Church. Made up of both men (captains and lieutenants) and women (sisters), this body was founded in England in the last century along lines similar to those of the Salvation Army. Today they devote themselves to evangelistic, pastoral, and welfare work, living at subsistence level in a truly Franciscan spirit.[26] In some respects, the Church Army resembles the deacons' brotherhoods of German Lutheranism.

In considering all of the special groups, organizations, orders, and societies which may possibly render assistance, it must be recalled that this assistance will not become available to the average parish until these orders and organizations receive wider recognition and encouragement, fuller support, and vastly more recruits. One hopes that this may come about in the future.

Where the people of a parish are actively working with their pastor at every level, where he has one or two deacons to help, and perhaps assistants from other special agencies of the church, it becomes possible to carry on a very extensive operation, at a high qualitative level, even with severely limited funds and inadequate buildings. Nonetheless, a certain limit will be reached. As this limit of effective work approaches, plans should be made for the formation of one or more new congregations in the area.

The Large and Prosperous Parish

We have said something of small and middle-sized parishes. Let us now look at the large parish. For a change, let it be the parish which already has many of the outward and material assets to which smaller churches sometimes aspire. What are the distinctive problems of ministering to church growth in the so-called successful parish?

"Successful parishes" usually have a substantial list of members. Although not all of these attend services too faithfully, their children are duly baptized and confirmed in the parish. Even if they marry persons of other religious backgrounds, or of no religion, they seem to marry in the church, and the other partner assents, at least nominally, to joining. Many new persons moving into the community will also affiliate themselves gladly with the successful parish. And so members flow in, and continue to flow in. Yet, after a certain point, the number of worshipers on Sunday ceases to increase, and may even decline. The membership rolls grow, but it is an open secret that this list in unrealistic. Here then, we are encountering another form of curtailed and frustrated church growth.

What exactly is happening in such a situation? An interesting English study of church growth indicates that in the congregation which has exceeded the optimum size for its circumstances and locality, just as in the congregation which is too far below optimum size, the hold of the church on the interest and loyalty of many of its members declines.[27] In the large church new people come in each year, but they are matched by others who more or less lapse. The web of personal associations and contacts which holds the congregation together has been stretched too thin; the parish is faced with more individuals than it can minister to. There is in effect a kind of rotating membership. Some come and others go; some come back again; some take a turn in other parishes or in other denominations. In a community where this is widespread, there is an increasing number of nominal but virtually nonpracticing Christians. The newly confirmed are immediately demoralized by the example of friends or relatives who regard themselves as leading members of the parish, but who no longer go to church regularly. The zealous and devoted are disillusioned by constant contacts with respected but virtually inactive church people. After a long period of this, to revitalize the church is not easy. It is like trying to grow flowers in a garden where the soil has become rancid.

In such a parish the physical plant is not the problem; it is usually more than adequate. In larger parishes, the rector or pastor is often assisted by a curate or assistant clergyman; sometimes by two. Yet the effective pastoral capacity cannot be increased. Why? First of all, increasing the number of persons employed by a church has only a limited relevance to growth. Within a certain situation where one clergyman can effectively minister to sixty fully active families, two clergymen will be able to handle perhaps one hundred. Doubling the clerical staff in no sense doubles the genuine pastoral capacity of one congregation. Three clergymen in this same situation could extend perhaps to one hundred and twenty. A third or fourth man would probably permit no effective increase at all, unless each be given distinct pastoral assignments to virtually separate congregations. Meanwhile, all these clergy require salaries, housing, office facilities, and supervision. This increases the administrative burdens on the pastor or rector to such an extent that with too many assistants his own capacity to minister to people is reduced. Extra ordained men may perform certain useful tasks, but they do not make one congregation capable of limitless growth. Many parishes have recognized this and use their resources to employ a director of religious education, or other professional lay person, instead of further assistant clergy who would be unproductive in the situation.

What is the answer? As with a smaller church, the assuming of fuller responsibility by lay people is of major importance. Second, again as in the smaller congregation, there is the diaconate. Two full-time clergy in a large parish, no less than one in a smaller parish, can and should be assisted by deacons. The enrichment and strengthening of the ministry by other personalities and nonclerical backgrounds, the local ties and interests of the local man, and the fact that the official structure of the church can be seen to extend itself— all these are highly important.

At the same time, big churches in their situations, no less than smaller churches in theirs, have their ceiling. Such a ceiling can be foreseen well in advance, and if the potential for growth is still apparent, the large congregation can lay plans for starting a daughter church. In the sort of situation we have described, the founding of a new congregation is not difficult. The curate or junior minister can be loaned temporarily, or even assigned permanently, to the new chapel or mission. Since the clergyman in charge of the mother church will have a deacon or two to help him, he will not be unduly handicapped for a short period. In some cases, this will be the time to consider whether one of the deacons, or perhaps someone else, should be ordained to undertake pastoral work, while continuing in his secular livelihood. Such a man may well be able to take charge of a new congregation for several years.

The program of systematic and continuous church extension, as here outlined, is in clear and deliberate contrast to the policy of consolidation which many church administrators urge. Certainly in situations of decline, and where entire populations have moved away, some consolidation may be necessary. Where there is, however, the potential for growth (as is usually the case), consolidation can have a most negative effect. It encourages larger buildings, more expensive equipment, and increased secretarial staffs, but it does not usually encourage an increase in the total number of practicing Christians in the locality. Consolidation all too often expresses a negative attitude toward evangelism. An interesting Swedish Lutheran study of church attendance on Sunday indicates that a single church in a large and populous area is apt to have relatively poor attendance. When this large parish is divided and one or two new churches are built, not only do these daughter churches attract their own congregations, but the attendance at the mother church can also improve.[28]

A more complicated situation arises when a large church, to which many people are attracted, is surrounded by smaller ones of the same denomination which do not seem able to grow. In such a case, it is evident that the clergy and leading laity of the whole group of parishes need to undertake a careful and honest review of their situation in the light of the principles of church growth. Those in the smaller congregations can gradually come to a more positive attitude in regard to extending and expanding their outreach. Likewise those in the larger congregation can come to see that they are gaining nothing by ushering into their rolls a procession of temporary Christians. Certain programs and activities can be undertaken on an interparochial basis. The use of some self-supporting clergy makes it possible to strengthen the ministry at points where it is most needed without putting a financial burden on those least able to shoulder it. A local deanery or presbytery, involving both clergy and lay representatives, is the natural framework for this sort of planning.

So far we have been talking about classes of situations, without going too deeply into any specific examples. In the next chapter, however, we will take one extended example, in which most of the methods here discussed were actually tried in a single area for a number of years.

4

THE EVANSVILLE
ASSOCIATE MISSION:
A DECADE OF CREATIVITY

In the year 1932, a young clergyman named Joseph Moore moved from Illinois to southwestern Indiana, to assume charge of St. Paul's parish in Evansville. He did so at a time when the activities of the church, and of many other institutions, were nearly at a standstill. For the great depression had decimated the economy of mid-America. The steps which he and the people of his congregation took during the next ten years provide a remarkable example of a church being revitalized, and extending its ministry and witness to growing numbers of people in a widening area. This involved many of the procedures discussed in the present book, and did so in a rather striking manner, which this chapter will record in concrete and factual terms.

This case study has been chosen for several reasons. First of all, the story itself has a personal warmth and intrinsic interest of its own, although it has never before been recorded. Second, it was long enough ago to be viewed with objectivity and historical perspective. Many pastoral experiments have of course been conducted in many places more recently, but in recent cases the long-run effect may be questioned. Quite specifically, it is sometimes said that clergymen who are trained and ordained within the context of such experiments may be of limited competence at other times or in other situations. In the case of Evansville, however, such questions need not be left to speculation. Men and women who lived through these years now look back on them after a quarter of a century has passed. Clergy trained at Evansville have subsequently had full and useful careers in the ministry in the North, South, East, and West. In the present chapter, these matters are examined in some detail and specific information about the principal persons is given. Finally, the examination of a case of a generation ago has one unique advantage. When such proposals as are made in this book are put forward, many people believe that they can be carried out only in the future, after long preparation, and in specially favorable circumstances. The Evansville experience shows that such things have in fact been possible for many years, in a most typical American environment, in a conservative region, and at a time of severely limited resources.

Much of this story centers around the Rev. Joseph Graessle Moore. A native of Iowa, he grew up in Minnesota. After deciding to enter the ministry, he took his theological training in Evanston, Illinois, and was ordained in the Episcopal Church. He was married to the former Ruth Clare Shaughnessy. He subsequently served as an assistant in a large parish in Evanston for two years.[1] In southwestern Indiana he was called to be rector of St. Paul's Church, an old Episcopal congregation. With this our narrative begins.

Evansville and Its Environs

Evansville was at that time a city of over a hundred thousand people, located on the banks of the Ohio River about one hundred miles west of Louisville. Then, as now, it was a center for transportation in the surrounding region. The city also had a range of businesses and industries, among which the manufacture of furniture and of machinery were important. In the cultural life of the city, Evansville College (now a century old) has played an important part. In those days, it had several hundred students each year. Evansville had its wealthy and eminent families, its middle class and commercial folk, and a considerable number of laboring people, including some Negroes. The least privileged portion of the population was a group of poor families living on the west side in a tumbledown settlement of cottages and shacks. To the east of the city, a new suburban area was beginning to stretch out. Evansville thus presented a wide range of city life. It was in many ways a microcosm of urban America.

St. Paul's parish[2] had been founded by the great missionary bishop, Jackson Kemper, in 1837. In the 1930's, the parish occupied a large Victorian Gothic church, with a chapel and rectory[3] nearby, located in an old residential area not far from the river. It numbered about 400 communicants. There had been another smaller Episcopal church, Holy Innocents', located in the downtown area, but it had been closed a dozen years before and its parishioners assigned to St. Paul's. There were, of course, the usual range of other Protestant church groups found in any midwestern city, also Roman Catholics, and a small Jewish community.

Viewed in a slightly larger setting, Evansville is the metropolis of southwestern Indiana, sometimes known as the "pocket." [4] It is a roughly triangular area, wedged between Illinois and Kentucky. It is divided from the former by the Wabash River, which joins the Ohio about thirty miles southwest of Evansville. The broad, muddy stream of the Ohio itself, following a winding course to the southwest, divides the pocket from Kentucky. Henderson, situated several miles south of Evansville, is the major town in this part of Kentucky. The area as a whole is basically agricultural, yielding corn, cattle, and other products. Here and there small oil wells bring in extra income to landowners. There is also coal. In the half-dozen counties which constitute southwestern Indiana, there are several market and manufacturing towns, and four of them had small Episcopal churches. The area falls within the Episcopal Diocese of Indianapolis.

This then was the southwestern corner of Indiana; this was, and is, a typical corner of America.

Revitalization and Expansion in the Parish

The records of St. Paul's Church indicate that the new rector undertook an energetic program from the start. In November, 1932, a Boy Scout troop was formed. Girl Scouts were organized at the same time. Later a Sea Scout organization appeared, a club for young men, a chapter of the Brotherhood of St. Andrew (an evangelistic association for men), and various other groups. An institute was also organized to train Sunday school teachers from St. Paul's and from the nearby towns of Henderson, Kentucky, and New Harmony, Indiana. On May Day, 1934, the rector announced that preliminary steps were being taken to found a mission on the growing east side of the city. Property was soon acquired and two years later a small church was organized. (The first service in Epiphany Mission was held on January 10, 1937.)

Plans were also inaugurated for another mission to the west, in the poverty-stricken quarter already referred to. For this purpose the Social Welfare Guild was formed, and a man from the Church Army was brought in to head this work. Captain Frederick W. Brownell [5] was the first of a succession of Church Army men who played an outstanding role in the work in Evansville. The parish paid forty dollars a month for his support. A small disused chapel in the rundown neighborhood was first rented, and later purchased for a small sum by St. Paul's parish. This became Good Shepherd Mission and Neighborhood House. In addition to weekday services in the chapel, there were held here a Bible class, a prenatal and baby clinic, a hot-lunch program for children, an arts and crafts program, and a variety of other activities. Looking back in later years, Dr. Moore wrote:

It was a period in America's history when money was scarce, but lives were abundant, and the men and women of this parish gave their money and their time and energy. The congregation saw itself as a missionary community serving the whole city and area of Southwest Indiana, and did its best to answer its opportunity.[6]

The Extension and Expansion
of the Ministry

But what of the surrounding area? Two nearby towns, New Harmony and Mount Vernon, had shared a priest who left in the fall of 1932. Two other towns also had Episcopal churches, but none of these now had sufficient funds to employ a clergyman, nor was the Diocese of Indianapolis in any position to help during these lean years. This left the Rev. Joseph Moore the only Episcopal priest in the whole of southwest Indiana. He attempted to visit these outlying communities for occasional services, but he soon realized some more ambitious plan had to be undertaken to maintain these congregations.

The seeds for such a plan had already been sown. Before coming to Evansville, Father Moore had learned of the Omaha Associate Mission, which had operated a few decades before in Nebraska. Within this organization, a few men worked as a team to minister to several congregations.[7] Moore conjectured that a similar arrangement might meet the needs of the situation in southwest Indiana.

The first step was to recruit several laymen in Evansville who agreed to give one evening a week to study and to give every Saturday evening and Sunday morning to visiting the outlying towns and conducting services there. They also helped in the expanding program in Evansville itself. These lay readers, together with the Church Army captain and the rector, were formally constituted by the bishop as the Evansville Associate Mission, with Joseph Moore as director. This body was given charge of the work of the Episcopal Church in the entire area.[8] With the help of these men, a regular schedule of weekly services was restored in the four outlying churches. The rector visited each one periodically for the administration of the sacraments. It was soon apparent, however, that this was not yet an adequate arrangement, particularly in view of the expanding work in the city of Evansville. Moore read Roland Allen, and he too was convinced of the need for a fully ordained ministry. It was decided to extend the training of the lay readers so they might qualify for ordination to the diaconate and then the priesthood.

The oldest of the three original ordinands was Alfred Sanford Byers. He had twenty-five years of experience in teaching, and at this time was principal of Stanley Hall Public Elementary School in Evansville. He also had long experience as a choirmaster. He was ordained a deacon in July, 1933, and became a priest a year later.[9] The speed with which he was trained is worthy of note. His church duties were largely in Evansville, at St. Paul's, where he served as assistant priest and as choirmaster, but he also visited Cannelton regularly. After leaving Evansville, Father Byers undertook a period of graduate study during 1940 and 1941 and was with the Air Force during World War II. After being rector in Columbus, Indiana, for nine years, he retired in 1957. He died in 1962, after a fruitful ministry of a quarter of a century.

Next was Imri Murden Blackburn, Ph.D., Professor of Classics in Evansville College. An accomplished musician, he conducted the Civic Choral Society and took the college choir on yearly concert tours in the state. He and his wife had come to Evansville in 1932. With his academic background, Blackburn likewise quickly completed his training for ordination. He was ordained a deacon in June, 1934, and priest the following December. For over a year he then ministered regularly in the town of New Harmony, while continuing in his position at the college. In 1937 he was called to be rector of the parish in Henderson, Kentucky, and resigned from his secular work. He remained in Henderson until he became rector of St. Paul's, Evansville, in 1943. In 1954 Dr. Blackburn became Professor of Church History at Seabury-Western Theological Seminary in Evanston, Illinois. In 1960 he was appointed to the same chair at Nashotah House, a seminary in Wisconsin. He retired in 1966. His career is good evidence that the training of men for ordination in local communities does not lower the total intellectual level of the Church.

The third to be ordained was Raymond Stanley Ottensmeyer. A former Roman Catholic, he had several years earlier attended St. Meinrad College and its theological seminary,[10] but had finally decided not to pursue ordination in the Roman Catholic Church. He married, and worked in Evansville as a butcher in a local grocery. Having become an Episcopalian and having served as a lay reader in the Associate Mission, he was ordained a deacon at the end of 1935, and continued for some time in his secular employment. He was admitted to the priesthood in June, 1937, at New Harmony, where he remained in charge for the next two years. He too had great success with a boys' choir there. He was called to be rector in Greenville, Ohio, in 1939. Father Ottensmeyer later served churches in Texas, Minnesota, and northern Wisconsin. He has filled various positions of responsibility in dioceses in which he has served, and has twice been a deputy to the General Convention of the Episcopal Church.

All three of these men were natives of Indiana, and all were ordained by the Rt. Rev. Joseph Marshall Francis, who was reaching the end of his forty-year episcopate (1899–

1939) in the Diocese of Indianapolis. All three of these men happened to have had college educations, and hence there was no formal academic obstacle to their immediate pursuit of theological study. Other men also served as lay members of the Associate Mission and began their preparation for Holy Orders, but were not ordained until some years later.

Frank Marchal Butler served as a lay reader during the mid-1930's, graduated from Evansville College in 1940, and was then employed for a brief period as a lay assistant at St. Paul's. During most of this period he was supporting himself as a printer and commercial artist in Evansville. After World War II, he was ordained in the Diocese of New York. For several years he then served the churches in West Park and Highland, New York. South Florida has been the scene of his subsequent ministry, where he has been successfully engaged both in pastoral work and in teaching. Father Butler's artistic talents have been utilized in illustrating various religious publications.

Samuel Nathan Keys was a young salesman of paper products in Evansville, and served as a lay reader during the mid-1930's. He was assigned to serve mainly in the church in Cannelton. He later went to southern Ohio and was ordained there. He served parishes in Ohio and more recently in Illinois. During the 1950's he had a leading role in diocesan, provincial, and national organizations for stimulating and developing the Church's work in small towns and rural areas.

Several others had similar roles at St. Paul's for brief periods. Among these was William Douglas Winn, a student from Georgia whom Father Moore arranged to have come to Evansville during the latter part of this period. He attended the college and received board, lodging, and a small salary for working in the church. Some years later he received seminary training and was ordained in the Diocese of Atlanta, where he has continued to serve. Frederick J. Haskin, later ordained in Chicago, joined in the work of the Associate Mission when visiting the Moores from time to time. Another worker was Milton Moore, a Lutheran student later ordained as a Lutheran pastor. The fact that these men could proceed from Evansville to positions where the tone and character of church life were so different is ample indication that the Evansville program did not lead to a narrow or stereotyped outlook.

There were no permanent deacons ordained, but the diaconate was recognized as a period of useful ministry on the way to the priesthood. All of the men who were deacons were given very full roles, and greater responsibilities than were customary in this period. Besides those trained in the parish, the Rev. John T. Williston, a recent seminary graduate, was employed as an assistant at St. Paul's during his diaconate in 1935 and 1936. The Church Army, however, did provide a rank of officially recognized assistants in the work of the Church. A series of Church Army captains were sent to Evansville as their first assignment after graduating from their training. They made an invaluable contribution. They were normally assigned to the Good Shepherd Mission, but also worked in the other churches of the area. In later years, some of these men left the Church Army in order to enter the priesthood.

It is not to be supposed that the clergy, lay readers, and Church Army captains of the Associate Mission did their work alone. Both in the city and in the outlying towns, the men and women and the boys and girls helped in all sorts of ways, as we shall see. For dozens of them, the activities centering around St. Paul's were a major focus in life during these years.

The Other Towns and Their Churches

The towns which the Associate Mission served were an interesting cross-section of small town and rural life.

About twenty miles west of Evansville was Mount Vernon,[11] with a population of several thousand. It was essentially an agricultural center, with food-processing works and small manufacturing; a quiet, prosperous, hard-working little world, where prior to the present decade changes have come very slowly. St. John's Church, erected in the middle of the last century, was a small wooden building of rustic Gothic. Immediately before the period under consideration, the priest from New Harmony had ministered here. Under the Evansville Associate Mission, Mount Vernon seems to have become the special responsibility of Raymond Ottensmeyer. Later on, when the Rev. G. W. Smith came to New Harmony, he, like his predecessors, also served Mount Vernon. This arrangement was maintained until more recent years. Today Mount Vernon has a resident vicar and a growing congregation.

Proceeding north for twenty miles we come to New Harmony. If anyone supposes that midwestern villages are colorless and uninteresting, they will find this place a shock.[12] The background is so unusual that it requires a fuller account. "Harmonie," as it was first called, was founded on the banks of the Wabash in 1814 by the followers of Father George Rapp, a German Pietist and utopian reformer. The Rappites were for the most part celibate and resembled the Shakers. Here on the very edge of the American frontier, they built a group of remarkable buildings and established an affluent community marked by extraordinarily advanced technology and scientific agriculture. In 1824 their vast tract of land and the buildings were purchased by the British philanthropist and social reformer, Robert Owen, with the assistance of William Maclure, another philanthropist. They brought in a whole new utopian colony, recruited from all over Europe, to constitute "New Harmony." This group lacked the manual and agricultural skill to maintain the productivity of the village. The communitarian constitution was progressively abandoned within a few years, and Robert Owen returned to

Britain. Maclure and many others remained, including Owen's sons, Robert Dale Owen, statesman and founder of the Smithsonian Institution, and David Dale Owen, the great geologist. Throughout the middle of the last century, New Harmony remained a remarkable cultural center. By the end of the century, however, it was simply a rural village, marked by some unusual old buildings, some proud memories, and the distinguished names of several of its families. For most of its history, its population has numbered around one thousand.

Although Robert Owen was opposed to organized religion, some of his followers were Anglicans, and Bishop Kemper visited New Harmony in 1838. St. Stephen's Church was organized in 1841 and soon afterward it was given part of the vast old Rappite church building as a place of worship. A decade later new land was bought, and an Episcopal church building was erected. In 1912 this was replaced by the present church, an undistinguished edifice of concrete masonry. From then until the 1930's, the parish was served by several clergy, with greater continuity, it seems, than has usually been the case for small communities.[13] The Associate Mission assumed responsibility in 1934. Captain Brownell took charge for a brief period, until St. Stephen's was assigned to Dr. Blackburn, who came out regularly from Evansville for a year and a half. During the summer of 1935, he resided in New Harmony. From the spring of 1936, Raymond Ottensmeyer took charge for three years. By 1937 St. Stephen's was no longer dependent on Evansville, and Ottensmeyer was succeeded by the Rev. George Washington Smith who remained a decade and then moved to Cannelton. In more recent years, the interest in New Harmony's unique history has increased. Through the generosity of various benefactors, the older houses are gradually being restored, and significant new buildings erected. Religion has been given an important role in the renaissance of New Harmony, and today the priest at

St. Stephen's in effect serves also as a chaplain to the growing program of educational and cultural activities in the community.

Continuing clockwise around the area, we next come to Princeton, a market town of several thousand people about twenty-five miles north of Evansville. This had had for some years a small Episcopal congregation, St. Andrew's, which had been served by the priest from nearby Vincennes. During the period we are discussing it was assigned to the Evansville Associate Mission. It did not respond to stimulation, however, and it continued with only a handful of people until the work was given up in the 1940's.

Moving to the east, the next town with an Episcopal church is Cannelton,[14] located on the north bank of the Ohio River halfway to Louisville. The town takes its name from the cannel coal once excavated here, and it was settled by New Englanders, together with some Germans and French. Before the Civil War a cotton textile business had been established here and the huge castlelike mill still rises up in the middle of town, dominating the whole community with its dark stone masonry. Today a plastics textile factory is housed within its walls. With its cluster of small shops, its dusty streets, and modest houses around the old mill, Cannelton looks not unlike a small New England factory town.

St. Luke's Church in Cannelton is a white clapboard building, standing on a little hillock near the middle of town. Since it was erected in 1845, Unitarians, Roman Catholics, and Methodists have all worshiped here for short periods, until an Episcopal congregation acquired the building a little over a century ago. Today, a much larger Roman Catholic church looks down from the hillside farther up from the river. In little more than a century, St. Luke's has been served by twenty-eight different clergy, as well as by various lay readers and Church Army captains. In the lack of sustained and continuing pastoral leadership, it is typical of many small churches.[15] Within the Associate Mission, Alfred Byers seems to have been especially responsible for Cannelton. Both Samuel Keys and Frank Butler worked there also. Later on, Cannelton was assigned to Captain John L. W. Thomas,[16] who worked at the Good Shepherd Mission in Evansville during the week, and then proceeded to Cannelton by bus on Friday afternoon. He would remain there until Sunday afternoon, thus having time to call on parishioners and offer pastoral leadership, as well as giving his attention to the Sunday school and the service of worship on Sunday morning. The Rev. Raymond O'Brien, an assistant clergyman in Evansville during the latter part of the period, came out to Cannelton one Sunday a month for the administration of the sacraments. In the early 1940's, like the other smaller communities, Cannelton was feeling the loss of young people who were going into military service or to jobs in defense industries. It is only in recent years that new opportunities for employment—especially those provided by the building of a massive dam across the Ohio—have both held young people and attracted some newcomers into the neighborhood. Cannelton today remains a quiet little community of about 1,800 souls. St. Luke's has its own priest, residing in a suburb where newer homes are being built.

Evansville was, and is, a miniature "big city." The other towns represent various types of smaller conservative communities. The Evansville Associate Mission carried these small churches through an era of hardship, and re-established a resident vicar in one of them (New Harmony). In the person of Samuel Keys, the Mission contributed a leader to the rural field at large. It remains regrettable, however, that in this period it was not found possible to train local leaders, within these outlying towns themselves, to assume greater responsibility for these small congregations. It probably could have been done in one or two cases in the changed conditions of the postwar years.

Later Developments in Evansville

The breadth and width of the outreach of St. Paul's parish was startling. If it is sometimes supposed that attention to local missions and church extension curtail a parish's concern for immediate human needs, the evidence of Evansville does not support such fears.

The parish house became the headquarters for the Non-Partisan Citizens' Association for Clean Elections. This organization undertook to expose and combat the scandalous abuses that had been taking place at the polls in Evansville, and it entered into many controversies. In 1940 Captain Thomas made photographs of political workers actually handing money to voters near a poll, and he was attacked by thugs in retaliation. The Association finally had the satisfaction of seeing extensive reforms undertaken. A zone organization was established to assign families from the church to neighborhood social service work throughout the city.[17] St. Paul's is believed to have been the first large white church in Evansville to welcome Negro membership. An interracial committee begun in the parish later led the city to establish a permanent commission for racial justice. Members of the parish also became involved in labor-management affairs. Several parishioners had leading roles in public life and were elected to important positions of responsibility. Inspired by the generous social philosophy of Archbishop William Temple, the American Committee on the Malvern Movement had its headquarters in Evansville in the early 1940's. The leaders were the rector of St. Paul's, the Rev. Joseph F. Fletcher of Cincinnati, and Mr. Stanley Matthews of Glendale, Ohio. This organization continued for several years, and sponsored meetings and conferences in several parts of the country. The parish also helped a number of refugees from Europe.

The worship of God was not overshadowed by the many organizational and social activities of the parish. Although the schedule did not remain the same throughout the decade, during most of the period we are considering, Morning and Evening Prayer were recited daily in the large chapel adjoining the parish church, and Holy Communion was celebrated several times each week. After supper on Saturday evening, there was a service of prayer and meditation in preparation for Holy Communion the next day. A number of more devout people attended this Saturday evening service regularly. On Sunday morning, there was the service of Holy Communion at eight o'clock, and at eleven o'clock there was a Choral Eucharist and sermon on the first Sunday of the month and on special feasts, and Morning Prayer and Sermon on the other Sundays—as was customary in many Episcopal parishes in this period. Moore introduced an additional Choral Eucharist at nine-thirty every Sunday, at which one of the lay readers always read the Epistle, and a deacon if there was one, or one of the priests, came forward to the head of the nave to read the Gospel—all of which was unusual in those days, although almost everywhere recognized as desirable today. In the latter part of the decade, a simpler celebration of the Eucharist was added at 12:10 on Sundays. Evensong and sermon took place every Sunday afternoon.

Moore was a dynamic preacher, and many eminent clergy of the period were also invited to come as preachers from time to time. One such frequent visitor was the Rev. Gilbert P. Symons, of Cincinnati, one of the founders of the Forward Movement. It was under his influence and guidance that a number of cell groups were founded, with "prayer, study, action" as their watchwords. From these cells much of the planning and leadership for the various parish and community activities emanated.

Undoubtedly one of the most attractive features of St. Paul's, which was much appreciated by the people, was the

liturgical music. This of course reflected the musical competence of several of the clergy. The rector's own talents as
a singer were fully utilized in the choral services. There were
three choirs, for the nine-thirty, eleven o'clock, and afternoon services respectively. On special occasions, unusual
music was undertaken. An annual event was the singing of
a Gounod Mass at the midnight service at Christmas. For
Christmas and Easter the local high school orchestra (led
by a parishioner) came to the church to provide the accompaniment. Today the religious music of Gounod is not
regarded as "liturgical" in the stricter sense, yet a mass of
this magnitude, performed not in a concert but in an actual
service of worship in which a large congregation was par-
ticipating and communicating, provided a most memorable
experience.

Regular church attendance was strongly and successfully
emphasized at St. Paul's. A lay volunteer organized a committee to check the attendance at every Sunday service
against the roll of parish membership. Those who missed
services were promptly contacted. Needless to say, persons
prevented by illness or other difficulty appreciated the attention, whereas those who had no such excuses were quickly
reminded that worship is a duty not to be forgotten. Amid
the innumerable "secular activities" of the parish, the ultimate spiritual motivation was clearly affirmed in corporate
worship.

Various educational and cultural programs were constantly
being undertaken. We have seen the stress on music. Mrs.
Moore was much interested in drama, and numerous amateur
performances were produced under her direction. Some were
religious dramas, others were not. Frank Butler, it is recalled,
was regularly featured as a villain. From these plays, a Little
Theater organization emerged in Evansville and has continued. The great number of special organizations for boys
and girls have already been alluded to, but there were also

dances and other social activities for teenagers and young adults at Christmas and other times.

Ecumenical activities included discussion groups with other Christians and with Jews. Moore was himself closely associated with other Protestant and Catholic clergy and the rabbi. Long before the present vogue for ecumenism, interfaith religious discussions were being broadcast by radio in Evansville.

All sorts of schemes were tried to raise money, and the rector was constantly on the point of taking a secular job to support himself. Because the rectory was large, it was divided into two apartments. The Moores and their three boys lived in one; the other was rented. On the same street, immediately beyond the rectory, two old houses were bought. These had some apartment space for rental, and a number of rooms in which men working in various parish projects lived, so that they might subsist very economically—a degree of economy, indeed, which some found too Spartan.

In January, 1937, a great flood wrought havoc in the Ohio valley, and Moore, like many other clergy and lay people, worked heroically in rescue and relief work. The basement of the church was flooded and the electrical insulations damaged, but the extent of the damage was not appreciated at the time. It was the next year, 1938, that the results became apparent. Damage to the wiring eventually caused a fire which completely gutted the inside of the great church. Sunday services were held in the parish hall while the entire interior of the church was reconstructed. It was done in an attractive neo-Gothic style of that era. Unlike many parish churches, St. Paul's had had adequate and up-to-date insurance coverage.

All of these things were going on in a time of poverty, and in a parish which, in the earlier part of this period, operated on considerably less than $15,000 per year. Many of these activities were controversial, and much resistance had to be overcome. All involved much hard labor. It was of course a faithful few who provided the spark of leadership and it was they too who also had to toil the most . . . the hours of supervision of children, the mimeographing of the parish newspaper in the late hours of the night, the answering of calls at all hours, the endless patching and pushing and improvising. Special mention should of course be made of the women who did secretarial work and so much else besides during these years and later, persons such as Mrs. Ann K. Harris, Miss Maxie E. Allman, and Miss Juanita Spencer. There were headaches, but also much joy.

Parishioners still remember the living room of the parish house in the middle of the night, unkempt and the furniture battered, perhaps with a professor from the college leading a discussion of philosophy at one end, and a Viennese musician talking German with friends at the other end. At such times Father Moore would come in, his clothes wet and disheveled, bringing in an intoxicated tramp from the alley to spend the night. Those were nights when heaven dipped low over Evansville.

Southwestern Indiana was of course not an island unto itself. Through the rector, the congregations we have been considering were very actively related with the Diocese of Indianapolis and with the Church at large. Moore had become recognized as a leading priest within the diocese, and to some extent within the neighboring dioceses. During most of this period, he was the head of the diocesan Department of Missions. He was three times elected a deputy to the triennial General Convention of the Episcopal Church, and twice served as a delegate to the Provincial Synod of the Midwestern dioceses. Father Moore also had close links with the Diocese of Southern Ohio, which was one of the most active and influential in the United States in this period. He and Captain Thomas were among the first to embark on an itinerant tour in the trailer-chapel called the Wayside Cathedral of Southern Ohio.

It cannot be claimed, however, that the relationship with his own diocese was entirely happy. In the first years, when the diocese was drastically handicapped by lack of funds and personnel, Moore's work was applauded, and Bishop Francis gladly encouraged the Associate Mission. Later on, however, as the economy improved, the manifold activities and programs at St. Paul's began to be viewed with some suspicion. In his diocesan responsibilities, Moore naturally and inevitably held some views which differed from those of the aged bishop, and the latter became less enthusiastic about what was happening in Evansville. The aspect of the Associate Mission most easily curtailed was the distinctive apprenticeship and training system whereby men became lay readers, then deacons, and then priests. A man cannot even approach ordination in the Episcopal Church without the approbation and encouragement of his bishop. During the latter part of the period such approbation and encouragement ceased to be extended to members of the Mission, and the men trained for ordination in these years were ordained only after moving elsewhere.

Meanwhile, it is only fair to say that by the late 1930's, the economy of the nation had much improved, and parishes were now looking for clergy to employ. It was supposed that the "normalcy" of the 1920's would return. Not foreseeing the permanent character of the social changes which were occurring, people supposed that expedients which had been undertaken in the times of hardship would no longer be necessary. A self-supporting ministry was not understood or appreciated in the Church at large. New Harmony and Mount Vernon, as we have seen, were now able to have a resident priest shared between them, and St. Paul's was in the position to hire a full-time curate also.

By 1939, the period of a self-supporting ordained ministry was over, although lay workers and Church Army captains continued to work with Moore in the Evansville Associate Mission. Father Ottensmeyer had gone to Ohio, and Dr. Blackburn had gone to Kentucky two years before, and now Father Byers withdrew for a period of graduate study. The Rev. Raymond M. O'Brien was engaged in 1939. He was given the following instructions:

Your duties will include a service each Sunday afternoon, and one trip a month on a weekday to Cannelton. As Assistant Rector of St. Paul's you will have charge of the training and development of our three choirs, together with active duty as resident [superintendent] of the Good Shepherd Neighborhood House activities, and the usual pastoral activities with young people, and educational classes of the Parish as a whole.[18]

Father O'Brien remained two years and then went to West Park, New York.[19] Then St. Paul's had to look again largely to lay leadership of its activities. In 1941 Cannelton was put primarily under Captain John Thomas, while he continued to work during most of the week at the Good Shepherd Mission on the west side of Evansville. Douglas Winn was engaged on a small salary as a lay assistant to work in Epiphany Mission on the east side.[20] The next year Frank Butler was employed as a lay assistant at St. Paul's. A few years later, after moving to New York and being ordained, he was to succeed Father O'Brien at West Park.

In 1942, the story was drawing to a close. Evansville was now flooded with young men in uniform. The rector was much concerned about them, and St. Paul's parish house soon became a servicemen's center and hostel. Men were welcomed every night of the week, and hostesses and counselors were provided—a program no other institution in the city equalled. Cots donated by friends were set up in the parish hall. When these were filled, men slept in the pews of the chapel, and even on the kitchen table. In the mornings, Miss Spencer and others made them a hearty breakfast. They could eat all they wanted for 25 cents. As many as sixty were served in a single morning.

Naturally many of the young men in the parish itself were going into the armed forces. After the Rev. Claire T. Crenshaw was engaged as an assistant, later in 1942, the rector himself left to enter the Army as a chaplain.

Thus ends the decade which we have attempted to chronicle. It will be of interest to consider very briefly some of the subsequent events. In the shadow of war, much of the program we have considered was curtailed and disbanded. Conditions in the west-side derelict area had much improved, and public agencies had taken over much of the necessary welfare work. Accordingly the Good Shepherd was closed under the pressure of the war years. Today, however, the chapel is again used by a local Protestant congregation— good evidence of the perennial ability of humbler people to maintain their own religious life. The Epiphany Mission to the east was also closed and the premises were sold soon after Moore's departure. The idea remained alive, however, and the financial assets of this mission were used a few years later to initiate St. Michael's and All Angels, which is now a growing congregation in the suburbs on the east side. Unfortunately, following Father Moore's departure, many who had disapproved of his activities became vociferous, and the vestry had some difficulty in maintaining the integrity of the parish. Order was restored when, after a brief interval, Dr. Blackburn was called from Henderson to be rector at St. Paul's, where he remained a dozen years before going into seminary work. The Rev. W. Robert Webb then left the deanship of the Cathedral in Bethlehem, Pennsylvania, to become rector of this parish. St. Paul's has continued to thrive. Today, southwestern Indiana is organized as a deanery, and the several congregations are again cooperating closely in an expanding program. It is interesting to note that a priest supporting himself in a skilled secular profession is again engaged in the area.

After World War II, Joseph Moore returned to Evanston, Illinois, where he undertook graduate work in sociology and anthropology at Northwestern University. He received the M.A. degree in 1947, and the Ph.D. in 1952.[21] During this period, he also served as an Assistant Professor in Seabury-Western Seminary. The methods he had developed for surveying the needs and opportunities of communities, and groups of communities, were implemented in the General Division of Research and Field Study of the Episcopal Church, of which Dr. Moore became the first Executive Director in 1950. The work he had carried on at St. Paul's was thus the foundation for the application of sociological knowledge to church planning and strategy, as it has since become known in much wider circles.

Conclusion

The achievements in Evansville from 1932 to 1942 illustrate what can be done by a clergyman, a very few employed assistants, and a host of ordinary people such as can be found in any American community, working with very limited economic resources. The program in Evansville reached out to the spiritual, social, intellectual, and physical needs of rich and poor. In some cases it was a temporary and local situation which was met; in other cases, these organizations and activities had a long life and made long-term contributions. Through the development of methods and the training of leadership, a rich contribution was made to the Church elsewhere.

Through the intensive use of lay workers, Church Army captains, and self-supporting clergy, the gospel could be preached, pastoral care given, and the sacraments administered in a large congregation and several smaller ones in a period of great economic hardship. Such a program, furthermore, was set up in a very short time. If the continuing and future need of self-supporting clergy had been more clearly and widely understood, and had had the bishop's approval, the training of additional men could have been continued indefinitely, in the opinion of Dr. Moore. Looking at it in retrospect, one may speculate that such a man as Dr. Blackburn might have been assigned to responsibilities of this sort, rather than local pastoral work. In the later part of our period, moreover, the rector himself was engaged in such a multitude of activities that it was no longer possible for him to give extensive attention to training men for ordination. Moore's increased involvement in local affairs was to some extent inevitable. This experience suggests that the establishment of a self-supporting auxiliary ministry in a congregation, or group of congregations, is something to be started as early as possible as a resource in a growing program. It cannot effectively be left to the end, as the climax of a program that has already achieved success and which has already overburdened everyone with responsibilities.

The exact circumstances at Evansville were to some extent unique. Yet the basic situation was simple—a large parish employing one clergyman, with several small churches located around it within a fifty-mile radius. This situation can be duplicated thousands of times, in all denominations, across the face of the continent, as well as in many other lands. Dr. Moore was certainly a leader with exceptional vision, but surely in all parts of the Christian Church today there are many highly able clergymen whose creativity could be allowed to blossom. The vast number of lay men, women, and children who made the program in Evansville possible were just such people as can be found in any comparable community. If St. Paul's had an unusual number of individuals with outstanding ability and zeal, it was because what went on in this parish attracted, held, and stimulated such people. What happened in Evansville can happen in countless other places.

5

WORSHIP

IN A LIVING CHURCH

The Christian mission is instigated by God. It must be carried out under his guidance and with his aid. As he is its beginning, so must he be its end: what the Church does must be offered to him, for his glory. These are the things which Christian worship expresses. The mission of the Church is ultimately the mission of God, who embodied it in the sending of his Son, Jesus Christ, into his world. The Scriptures which the Church reads, the hymns and prayers which it utters, and the sacred actions it performs are intended to unite us to Christ by the power of his Holy Spirit, so that we are made participants in his mission. As our Lord returned to the Father and ever lives to make intercession for us, so in worship all that we are and have is offered to the Father through him, our great High Priest. The rites of the Church are intended to express and embody the supernatural realities which are the very heart of the Church's mission. Accordingly, the Church which is serious about its mission must also be serious about its worship. Are the rites and practices of the Church, as they are in fact performed, actually accomplishing this? Is such a purpose being fulfilled?

These questions have a certain urgency, for it is primarily in attending the public rites of the local Christian community that most practicing Christians are consciously aware of their identity as members of the Christian Church. The services attended week after week, the words said again and again, the times of festivity and of penitence observed year after year—all these make an indelible impact not only on the conscious mind but on the feelings, loyalties, and underlying sentiments. The hour or more which so many millions of people spend in church every Sunday morning is precisely the time they wish to hear the Church's message, reaffirm its beliefs, and experience a sense of unity with their fellow believers in the performance of its services of worship. No other institution in our society involves so many people in an activity of this sort throughout their lives. For the Church to fail to make the most of this precious hour is precisely to forfeit a unique opportunity and privilege.

For those who attend church less often, the crucial importance of worship remains. Because of the dramatic nature of the occasion, services held on Christmas and Easter, or weddings and funerals, may make a deep impression even on persons with little religious perception. On the other hand, at such times a service that is poorly planned, or executed without sensitivity to the occasion, may also be remembered for many years—leaving a residue of hostility, misunderstanding, or cynicism.

As the Church moves forward toward new opportunities and achievements in a new age, it is of the utmost importance that the most sacred and yet most public rites of the Church give clear expression to the fundamental realities which we are seeking to affirm. In an old Church, in a conservative age, it may perhaps be assumed that most churchgoers understand the complicated doctrinal and symbolic structure with which religious observances are almost inevitably surrounded. In a renewed Church, in an age of rapid change, no such assumptions can be made. Neither new members, nor old members who have assimilated new ways of thinking, can be expected to understand or react positively to words and practices which have for them no significant relation to the matters at hand. All of this poses grave evangelistic and pastoral problems. Yet, as we shall see, both Scripture and liturgy continue to offer keys for solving the problems which they themselves raise. The public services and sacraments of the Church in fact offer abundant resources for expressing and implementing the things which have been discussed in the previous chapters. We shall consider these resources mainly in terms of two particular rites: Holy Baptism and the Holy Eucharist. The first provides us with an example of a special service performed from time to time. The second involves the slightly different problems relating to frequent and regular patterns of congregational worship.

Baptism in the Name of the Trinity

In considering church growth and local missionary activity, we have repeatedly seen the importance of lay initiative, lay activity, and lay responsibility. This is not merely a matter of pragmatic expediency. Rather, it stems ultimately from the theological conception of the people of the Church as living members of the Body of Christ, a royal and priestly people. This whole point of view finds its sacramental foundation in Holy Baptism. If Christian people are to see themselves, and one another, in such a light, the first and basic sacrament must be presented and administered in a manner congruent with the immense theological, psychological, and social weight that it must now bear.

The ultimate doctrine involved in baptism is the doctrine of creation, as it is affirmed in the beginning of the creed and in the beginning of the Bible. God made everything. Within his world he placed man as his viceroy, a creature that can stand upright and address his Creator—creation's spokesman to God and God's spokesman to creation. Among all the beautiful and wonderful things God made, Genesis pictures the man and woman as so pre-eminent that if one looked at them one would know what God looked like.

Second, baptism is concerned with the fact that humanity

has defected from its vocation and strayed from its potentialities. God accordingly sent his own Son into the world as a complete and perfect human being. At his baptism in the Jordan, it was revealed to him that he was the divine Son and the one anointed by the Holy Ghost, in short the Messiah or Christ, the Priest-King who would restore all things. The earthly phase of our Lord's royal priesthood was not exercised from a throne, or in the sanctuary of the Temple at Jerusalem. It was exercised on the paths and lanes of Gallilee, in people's homes and on fishing boats, in towns and cities, in meeting rich and poor, young and old, Pharisees and sinners, and in spending solitary nights in prayer. The royal priesthood of Jesus Christ was exercised in the fullness and completeness of the humanity of this one whole and perfect Man (Hebrews 2:11–18), and it reached its climax on earth in his death on the cross. After his resurrection and ascension, his royal priesthood has been exercised in another manner, and its earthly manifestation is in the lives of his followers.

Third, it is the work of the Holy Spirit thus to unite us to this perfect Man, Jesus Christ. In baptism we are made sharers of his divine Sonship and his spiritual anointing. The Spirit makes us partakers of his royal priesthood, so that we become a royal and priestly people through him.[1] Our royal priesthood, like his, is to be exercised in the fullness and wholeness of human life, and in bringing all this fullness and all this wholeness into the service of God—"whose service is perfect freedom." We are baptized so as to be united to Christ, which is to be authentically and genuinely *human*, as God created man to be. "Coming to him, as unto a living stone, . . . ye also as lively stones, are built up a spiritual house, an holy priesthood, to offer up spiritual sacrifices, acceptable to God by Jesus Christ" (I Peter 2:4–5).

Our restoration to God the Father, through the mediation of his Son, Jesus Christ, to whom we are united by the Holy

Spirit, is what we mean by baptism in the name of the Father and of the Son and of the Holy Ghost. This same meaning underlies the various other actions associated with baptism: the instruction in the faith given (in the case of older candidates) before baptism, the social incorporation into the Christian community which accompanies it, and the confirmation and first communion which follow it.

All of this may be familiar enough territory to the clergyman or theologically trained layman. But does an ordinary baptism, taking place in an ordinary American church today, really express all this, or anything like this, to the ordinary worshiper?

The conception of baptism as a restoration and renewal of one's proper role in creation is rarely alluded to. The words which the congregation hears at most baptisms hardly sustain such an idea. The beginning of the creed indeed affirms the importance of the doctrine of creation, but none except ecclesiastical historians realize that the creed was originally and properly a baptismal formula.[2] Current liturgical customs unfortunately do little to express the special relation of the creed to this sacrament. The story of creation in Genesis is not read at baptism except where the Easter vigil is restored, and this is certainly one of the great values in the restoration of the latter.

Theologians and anthropologists tell us that the primeval element of water itself is a symbol of creation, as doubtless it is. At the average baptism, however, the amount of water is far too slight to serve such cosmic imagery. Indeed, at the average public baptism, people see the clergyman, the candidates, and the sponsors, but do people standing a dozen yards away in fact see any water at all? They know that only the most trivial amount is employed. In many churches the font is so constructed that it simply could not hold enough water to have any dramatic force.

Our Lord's baptism is strongly emphasized in the four

Gospels, and has immense theological significance. The major churches which have retained a strong link in popular consciousness between Jesus' baptism and ours are the Baptists and the Eastern Orthodox. It is hardly coincidental that these are churches which have retained the ancient and once-universal practice of total immersion. In the traditional Western arrangement, as followed in many denominations, the account of our Lord's baptism is not read when the sacrament is administered. Although countless children are baptized every winter, few parishes of any denomination make any effort to schedule such baptisms at Epiphany-time when our Lord's baptism is liturgically commemorated.[3] Thus the opportunity for vivid, dramatic, popular identification is lost year after year.

Christian baptism, like the initiatory rites of certain other faiths, must be concerned with death. Death is a fundamental fact of our present earthly existence. Without facing it, one cannot be fully adult or fully human. No permanent communities exist until people have died for them. The risking of life in war, in childbirth, or in other ways has a central function in the sense of values of any society. The great Pauline interpretation of baptism as a mystical burial (Romans 6:3–11; Colossians 2:12) is familiar to Bible students. Preachers tell our congregations that baptism is like death and burial. Then they proceed to administer the sacrament in a way which is plainly *not at all* like death and burial. To perform rites in a way which betrays the interpretation given to them only makes the worshiper regard theology as a science of elaborate nonsense. One must also bewail the absence of effort, in so many cases, to restore baptism to the season of our Lord's victory over death. Easter must be the primary date for this sacrament.

Similarly, the role of the Holy Spirit can be affirmed by the administration of the sacrament at Pentecost, and by a closer association of baptism with confirmation. In most churches of the Western world, the ancient practice of confirming and communicating small children is not now permitted. Many baptisms today, however, involve older children and adults. Where the effort is made, in many cases it in fact is possible to have baptism, confirmation, and then the administration of communion to the newly confirmed and to the entire congregation.

The corporate character of baptism as the act of admission into the fellowship of the Church is much spoken of. In many areas, a successful effort has been made in recent years to curtail the administration of this sacrament in private homes and on weekdays, and to encourage its restoration as a public act performed during a service of congregational worship. This restoration of the public rite as the normal means of administering baptism has been a great step forward. Yet we still have much further to go. If baptism is simply administered at random on numerous Sundays of the year, many people will tire of its public administration and will be annoyed at the extra time it adds to the regular services of worship. The clergy naturally hope that with increasing familiarity, the theological significance of the sacrament itself will prove gripping—but it is neither likely, nor even desirable, that this should be sufficient. A clergyman is interested in theology, of course. The usual training and professional formation of a clergyman orient him toward verbal conceptions of spiritual matters. Lay people not only misunderstand theological and archaic terms, but in many cases they simply are not interested in reducing their convictions and deepest feelings to any such scheme of words at all. And why should they be? To a large portion of people, colors, shapes, odors, physical movements, and musical tones have more vivid and expressive power than words. For the Church to limit its highest expressions exclusively to words is ultimately to limit its effective membership to such persons as are oriented, by heredity, temperament, or training, to verbal patterns of thought. Total concentration on words excludes young children, deaf persons, recent immigrants, and the uneducated. In short it erects the kind of social and class barriers which the Church is specifically called upon to destroy. *Exclusive reliance on verbal communication destroys the catholicity of the Church.*

The dramatic character of baptism is enhanced by its periodic administration at seasons of the church year which have direct historical and doctrinal relevance. The font, and the area surrounding it, can be so decorated as to mark it out as a particularly holy and beautiful place.[4] At the great feasts and other times particularly appropriate to baptism, this area can be decorated with flowers, candles, and other embellishments. Baptismal candidates, sponsors, and officiating clergy can be escorted in procession to and from the font by processional cross and tapers. It is especially important that this great sacrament not appear as an individual action performed by one clergyman. When a deacon or other assistant clergyman is present, he should at least be given the privilege of reading the Gospel. When a bishop is present, he can preside over the entire rite, and express his sacramental participation by blessing the font;[5] then the parish clergy can apply the water to the individual candidates. When the rite is carried out by several of the clergy, people realize that a new Christian was not baptized by an individual minister, but by the Church.

When baptism is at once followed by confirmation and first communion, and all of these are performed in the context of a corporate rite in which clergy, lay readers, servers, choristers, and communicating congregation have their part, the result is extraordinarily impressive—in spite of its considerable length. In such a rite, the solemnity of the royal priesthood of every member of the Church is indeed made clear. It is all the more impressive on a major feast, and when cognizance can be taken of local events and circumstances.

Every baptism cannot be on this scale, but if some are each year, the prevailing outlook and attitude toward the sacrament will certainly be elevated.

Above all, more water must be used. The question of whether immersion is "necessary" is not the issue. The issue is whether we value baptism so much, and value Christian unity so much, that we will be eager to perform it in the way that cannot fail to be meaningful to the majority of Christian believers. Since all Christians regard immersion (or such a degree of affusion as wets the entire person) as a possible method of baptism, some regard it as a preferable method,[6] and many regard it as the sole method—it follows that immersion (or complete affusion, which comes to much the same thing) is the only method of baptism which can claim to be ecumenical.

At least in some years, could not bishops observe Pentecost, and other suitable feasts in the late spring and summer,[7] by visiting a congregation, or group of congregations, in a rural area in which there is access to a river, lake, or seashore? They could there preside, over out-of-door public baptisms in an open body of water, at a time of year when nature gives its own testimony to the doctrine of creation. The bishop could then confirm, and concelebrate the Eucharist with local pastors at a table under a canopy. A picnic luncheon would of course follow. For those who were present, this would be an event of a lifetime. Because of the dramatic character of the occasion, it would lend itself to being reported and relayed through the media of communication to a much larger public. The mere fact that such an event could take place from time to time would itself have great meaning.

Most Americans, of almost all churches, assume that the observance of a traditional liturgy, the recitation of a fixed creed, and the use of a sacerdotal ministry are all diametrically opposed to baptism by immersion, emphasis on the Bible, and acceptance of the religious folkways of the land. Different Christian groups have behaved differently for so many centuries that we now take for granted the dismemberment of what was once a single, unitary Christian tradition. We cannot put the scattered pieces back together by mere intellectual speculation. Rather, we need public acts in which the reassembling of the pieces is in fact demonstrated. In this particular case proposed, people can actually see baptism by immersion, as implied in the Bible and as beloved by millions of biblically oriented Christians, actually being performed in the context of traditional liturgical practice and the observance of the Church Year.

The Church that opens its heart and performs its sacred acts in a boldly pastoral and missionary manner will not only open its doors to church growth; it will also open its doors to the renewal and rejuvenation of its own inner life. By imaginatively exalting Holy Baptism, and the other rites closely connected with it, the Church proclaims to its own members, and to the world, the joy and the glory of sharing in the new humanity of Jesus Christ, to whom we are united by his life-giving Spirit.

The Weekly Worship of Baptized People

The public worship of the Christian Church rests on the same foundations as baptism, for it is as baptized people that Christians worship God. We are restored at the font to our Father and Creator, through Jesus Christ our Lord, to whom we are united by the Holy Ghost. Accordingly, in the fellowship of the Spirit, we undertake, through the high priestly mediation of Jesus Christ, to offer all that we are and have back to the Father. The corporate worship of the Church, in other words, expresses what it is to be a royal and priestly people, seeking with God to draw all things into God's Kingdom and to make them redound to God's glory.

In one sense, this should characterize the entire Christian life. But precisely because it is the intention and purpose of all life, it has to be summed up, articulated, and given conscious expression. It is the gift of God to us that as Christians we can experience such a summing up, such a point of unity, such a core of meaning, in the infinite and dazzling diversity of existence. Animals and plants glorify God simply by living their lives and carrying out their instinctive and chemically regulated activities. Man, on the other hand, has the unique privilege of living a self-conscious life, which can be knowingly and purposefully related to cosmic realities and an eternal destiny. The fully human life is precisely the life in which meaning, significance, and value are perceived, articulated, and expressed. This is part of the completeness of our manhood. To carry out this summing up of the basic purposes of our existence is the function of the Christian liturgy, the forms and patterns of worship which have emerged from the Bible and Christian experience. Such worship is sometimes very simple; sometimes very elaborate, utilizing all the resources of literary skill, music, color, architecture, and so forth.

An expression which does not express is nonsense. As we saw when discussing church growth, meetings which consistently fail to fulfill the purpose for which they are held will ultimately be attended only by persons who are animated by different motives. A growing church, a missionary church, must be ready and willing to make its true purposes and true commitments as evident as possible. In the regular conduct of public worship, just as in the periodic administration of baptism, a number of specific points can be mentioned.

The revindication of Sunday as the day of public worship deserves high strategic priority. The biblical association of the First Day with creation, the resurrection, and the gift of the Spirit needs to be clearly proclaimed in every congregation. We do not worship on Sunday because it happens to be a public holiday. In fact, at many periods of history, in many places, and for many people, it is not a holiday. Many people may prefer to take their holiday some other time. Baptized people observe Sunday, on the other hand, because it is the day of the Father, and of the Son, and of the Holy Ghost.[8] We assemble then to offer the first-fruits of creation to our Creator, to break bread with the Risen Lord, and to be renewed by the in-breathing of his Spirit. This needs to be clearly said. Even more important, it needs to be clearly done. The weekly worship of every church ought to have a plain and evident connection with the great biblical truths —not merely a connection perceptible to theologians and an inner circle of veteran members, but a connection evident to all who wish to see.

As we do not worship on Sunday because it happens to be a holiday, so we do not worship in church buildings because of their large size and usually elaborate appearance. A church building is primarily a convenient place for a number of people to assemble before a pulpit and around a table. Gracious decorations and significant works of art, where available, embellish the church and glorify the God of creation. Unfortunately, many churches of the last century appear to have been built in such a manner as to express mainly the prestige of the Christian community, and many churches of the present century appear to have been built to imitate those of the past century. The formation of congregations in small, poor, or transient communities should never be discouraged just because there are no resources for erecting or maintaining a building. The Christian Church is people, not masonry. A missionary Church must regularly demonstrate its ability to worship with dignity in simple secular buildings, and to sing the praises of God either without mechanical accompaniment, or with such musical instruments as may be locally available, such as the accordion, guitar, or saxophone. Every region or local area could benefit from having within it at least one duly constituted congregation which meets regularly on Sunday morning in a private dwelling, or in a restaurant, warehouse, or other conveniently available place.[9] All of us benefit from worshiping in such a setting from time to time.

The purpose of Christian worship needs to be reflected in the time and place of worship, but above all in the actual rite, or order of worship itself. From the earliest period of Christian history until the present, a comprehensive act of worship, including both word and sacrament, has been the characteristic Christian action on the Lord's Day.[10] This basic pattern appears in the records of the early Church and in the elaborate missals and other service books of the Middle Ages. During the Reformation it was asserted as normative by such leaders as Luther, Calvin, and Cranmer. Today, leaders in almost all parts of the Christian Church are recognizing the same basic pattern of weekly worship, and it is being expressed in almost all the recently revised orders of worship, among both Protestants and Catholics. Looking back, we can say all we wish about mistakes and abuses in the past, or the special historical backgrounds of certain Christian groups. It is time, however, that we face the fact that there is one, and only one, basic ecumenical pattern for weekly public worship—and then get on with the job.

In the years following World War II, it was the privilege of the Church of South India to demonstrate that this ancient and basic pattern of Christian liturgy can have a new vividness for our time. Although it consists largely of prayers already familiar to many English-speaking Christians throughout the world, the liturgy of South India[11] gives lucid articulation to the distinctive role of word and sacrament. It also felicitously combines the special leadership of the officiating presbyter with a very active participation of other assistants and of the congregation as a whole. The ecumenical origin of this liturgy is also significant. Much the same can be said of the eucharistic liturgy of the ecumenical Protestant monastic Community of Taizé in France.[12] A monastic body, devoting so much of its time and attention to corporate worship, naturally needs a more elaborate order than the mission congregations of South India. The basic structure of the rite, however, follows the same classic pattern, and again testifies to the power of liturgy as a meeting-ground for Christians of different backgrounds and traditions. At the other end of the ecclesiastical spectrum, Vatican Council II also manifested a dynamic concern for both ecumenicity and liturgical renewal.[13] It is a remarkable fact that the recent changes in the manner of performing the Roman Mass[14] have, in broad outline, followed very much the same pattern as that of South India a dozen years before—a most dramatic example of growing consensus.

In America today, governing bodies within both the Lutheran[15] and the Reformed[16] traditions have chosen official forms that are plainly based on the same classical and ecumenical pattern. Significant voices are also being raised in the Free Churches[17] for a closer adherence to historic standards. Throughout the English-speaking world, the Book of Common Prayer in its various editions in various nations has either been recently revised or revisions are being currently proposed.[18] In all of these cases, it is fair to say that liturgical revision has followed similar lines not merely because Christian leaders are seeking ecumenical norms, but because such leaders also are in fact convinced that the ancient pattern of word and sacrament does meet the needs of contemporary Christian people when they assemble in the Lord's name on the Lord's Day. The next step is for the rank and file of clergy and people in ordinary parishes to assimilate these new proposals and take advantage of the opportunities which they offer for fuller worship and fuller missionary action at the local level.[19]

Because the baptized are sharers in Christ's mission, seeking to bring all men to God through him, the first half of this basic pattern of worship centers in the proclamation of the Christian message. This first half of the Christian liturgy is sometimes called the Ministry of the Word. This is properly an evangelistic rite, in which the Good News is joyfully proclaimed, summoning unbelievers to the faith and summoning the faithful to fuller belief. Passages may be read from the Old Testament, and from the Epistles of the New Testament, and it is appropriate that laymen be appointed to read these. Psalms may be said and hymns sung. The climax of the Ministry of the Word is the reading from the Holy Gospels. The Gospel reading is not intended to manifest a doctrine or a moral, but to manifest Christ. He speaks to us, and makes himself known, as the Lord who is in the midst of his people. How do the customary passages portray him? Surely not primarily as a theologian or as a religious functionary, but as a man, as the Man, who came into the scene to speak, to touch, to heal, to judge, to liberate. So he described his own ministry: "Go your way and tell John what things ye have seen and heard; how that the blind see, the lame walk, the lepers are cleansed, the deaf hear, the dead are raised, to the poor the gospel is preached" (Luke 7:22).

It is this Jesus who frees people, who helps them to arise, who gives dignity and self-respect to all who turn to him— this Jesus who knows every man, who is the Lord and the Judge, and yet the Friend and Brother to every human soul —who seeks to meet us, touch us, and renew us. To declare this and show it to his hearers is the high privilege of the preacher.[20] Likewise in the prayers which follow, we seek to bring this power of Christ to bear on the lives of men. It is with Christ in our midst as our High Priest that we offer our intercessions through his name.

As the first half of the classical act of Christian worship is the Ministry of the Word, so the second half is the Ministry of the Sacrament. As the first is basically a simple action centering around the lectern or pulpit where the Bible is read and expounded, so the second half is also a basically simple action centering around the Holy Table, or altar, where bread and wine are taken, consecrated in a solemn prayer of thanksgiving, and distributed to the worshipers. Over the centuries, these simple actions have become embellished with stately words and music and ornaments. Certainly the Lord's Supper should have enough beauty about it to make it a festive occasion. A mission-minded church, however, will not allow the embellishments to become so elaborate that the simple basic structure is obscured. It is important, too, that this service never appear to be the monopoly of one man. Assistant clergy and representative lay persons should have consistently visible roles.

The centrality of the Lord's Supper in the weekly life of Christian people does not depend merely on its antiquity or on its ecumenicity. It stems, rather, from the fact that this service expresses, as none other can, the particular purpose for which we come together on the Lord's Day. This service is the formal assembly of those who have received the gift of the Spirit in baptism and confirmation and who continue "in the apostles' doctrine and fellowship and in breaking of bread, and in prayers" (Acts 2:42). Here we gather, as the first disciples did, to eat and drink with the Risen Lord. Here, through him, we offer to God the created tokens of the harvest of the world. In this rite, baptized people constantly experience their identity as the children of the Father, when they gather as his sons and daughters around his table. Here, as members of Christ, we are fed by his Body and Blood. And as the temple of the Holy Spirit we see this sacrificial action enacted in our midst.

In short, this is the service to which the great biblical truths about worship can be clearly, directly, and honestly related. A church which wishes to incorporate new members will rejoice in this clear, uninhibited biblical teaching. When liturgical worship is approached in this way, the dust of many old controversies can be swept aside. People who have truly met Christ in the Gospel and at the pulpit do not need to wait for any later "moment of consecration" in order to honor his real presence. He is in their midst, and the intercessions, offertory, consecration, and communion are all carried out in his company with him as High Priest. As he touched people, forgave, healed, liberated, and raised them up long ago, so we can find him, and be found by him, at his table now. Whatever teaching, or events, or aspects of our Lord's life are celebrated and read about on different Sundays and seasons of the year, each week the Eucharist becomes the sacrament of that doctrine or that event. The preacher helps us to discover this, and to share this discovery with our neighbors.

And so, to a praying people something happens. It is no longer necessary for the principal prayers to be said facing a wall, or for congregations to bury their heads in their pews. Worshipers do not have to fear to catch one another's eyes, nor to be heard singing. Christ helps people to be people. His humanity is contagious. He enables us to live and look out at the world and one another, as people—responsible, humble, self-respecting and other-respecting, loving. So, through him, we offer to our Father here, at this time, over this loaf and this cup, in conscious articulate terms, the thanksgiving which it is meet and right and the bounden duty of the entire universe, through all eternity, to offer up to its Creator.

The bread is broken, Christ's people are fed, and they go forth as his hands and his feet, to serve him in his world, for another week. The next week we return again, bringing back our small harvest of successes and failures to put them down at the foot of the cross, and to be sent out once more. As individual Christians, and groups of Christians, grapple in Christ's name with real problems, they discover, at an increasingly deep level, their need for his Word and his sacrament. In the multitude of problems life puts before us, people in particular situations will discover, as only they can, how their faith is to be expressed and applied. Yet these basic patterns of Christian living have an underlying simplicity which can be taught, by plain people, in plain speech. This the missionary Church must do. Living on these terms, we can go forth into the world in Christ's name. We will not be able to overcome all the pains, all the errors, or all the tragedies of life, but we will be able to face them as human persons who need be neither sorry nor ashamed to live and to die in this world, and in this age, in which God, in his infinite love, has seen fit to put us.

6

STARTING TODAY

Ideas such as we have been considering have been proposed in many quarters during the past few years. The present writer, like many lecturers, teachers, and conference leaders, has found a widespread willingness to accept these ways of thinking. Repeatedly, however, one runs into a certain type of query:

"This is wonderful, but how could we possibly do anything like this here?"

"I would like all of this, but wouldn't it require years of re-education before our people accepted it?"

"These things have to happen someday, but isn't it all too far ahead for us to worry about in a place like this?"

Such questions indicate a positive willingness to move ahead, coupled with a reluctance to start and an uncertainty as to *how to start*.

As for the reluctance, we can only repeat here what has been implied throughout these pages: If we had begun many years ago, we still would have been tragically late. All of these proposals are long overdue. As we saw in Chapter Four, it was in fact possible to do such things in a relatively conservative and impoverished region thirty years ago. Today, the Christian Church is in urgent need of moving forward everywhere. It may be questioned whether any congregation, in any locality, can now afford to stand on the beach for five years, or even for one year, before plunging into the salty but invigorating waters of Christian renewal.

The theological and intellectual questions surrounding Christian renewal have already been explored in an extensive and excellent literature on the subject. Whole mountains of words have been erected. Preliminary practical experiments have already been completed. It is time for the swimmers to begin to swim.

The question of *how to start* deserves a fuller answer, and to it we will devote the remaining pages. Basically, the answer —or answers—reflects the principle that *the nature of one's goal must be reflected in the methods one uses to attain that goal.* To promote interest in evangelism, one utilizes evangelistic methods within the Church to disseminate this interest. Lay initiative itself is the key to developing a more responsible laity. Involvement in a gripping experience of liturgical worship motivates people to desire liturgical reform. In each case, the objectives and results we are seeking must determine the means and techniques for reaching these results. This must never be lost sight of.

Prayer, Study, Action

One individual, a layman or a clergyman, can in fact begin the process of moving a congregation toward renewal. At the outset, such an individual should seek to associate several others with him, including, if possible, the rector, pastor, or minister of his parish. An easier step is always to enlist the support of a curate, junior priest, or assistant minister. Unfortunately, this easier step may have an adverse effect, as it may precipitate division within the parish administration and feelings of rivalry. Proponents of Christian renewal should make themselves known to the person at the top, and only with his approval and encouragement should they enlist his subordinates.

A small group is easily enough started in most localities.

What should such a group do? Like the Christian cells in Evansville, they can adopt the basic plan of "prayer, study, action." Since the renewal of the Church can be accomplished only by the Holy Spirit, the first thing we can do is to pray for the inspiration, guidance, and ardor of the Spirit. Members of a renewal group need to pray individually and collectively. From time to time, when they have an evening meeting in one of their homes or apartments, they can ask their clergyman to celebrate the Eucharist at the dining-room table, where they will subsequently sit down for supper or other refreshments. Thus they can induct him, and themselves, into a new and gripping sacramental experience. The experience of leading one or two such services can, by itself, revolutionize a clergyman's outlook toward the need for liturgical reform. By thus utilizing methods which relate directly to its goals, a renewal group can quickly precipitate interest in liturgical renewal.

As individuals become involved in a deeper practice of prayer and a more dynamic sacramental worship, they will be driven to the Bible and other Christian books which will help them explain and interpret their experiences to themselves and others. From the notes at the end of this book, and from other sources, one can learn of helpful books about Christian renewal. If such books are not easily available in the locality, a parish bookstall, or a parish lending library, may be initiated. Thus an important resource for adult education in the entire parish can be begun. Here again, the methods used by a renewal group can quickly bring results.

As prayer must soon be followed by study, so both must be promptly followed by some active project. All these must be continued *simultaneously*, although perhaps with a rotating cycle of emphasis. Many parishes have a prayer group which continues for years, as a great stimulus to spiritual development, but without commitment to a general renewal.

Similarly, a study group may usefully pursue its purposes for decades. A renewal group must not fall into this pattern, or ever allow itself to become domesticated as simply "one more parish organization" for a few people who like that sort of thing. Just as a renewal group may decide to initiate a parish library, so it might initiate a prayer guild or a reading club, but as soon as this other organization is on its feet, the renewal group itself should direct its attention to revitalizing some other phase of parish life. Renewal must never be exclusively identified with any one project or any single activity.

As it undertakes new projects, the renewal group must direct its prayers toward new topics, and its members must equip themselves with new kinds of information. Having started a parish library one year and a prayer guild the next, a renewal group might give its attention the following year to some welfare project in the local community, or an ecumenical activity, or something involving foreign missions. In every locality there are countless things that need to be done, if only someone has the imagination and the courage to undertake them.

This ongoing process of prayer, study, and action should be visibly marked by certain characteristics. First of all, it must not be secret. Promoters of Christian renewal should be glad to declare themselves and make their objectives known. Some of their activities, at least, should be publicized and open to the participation of all who desire to take part. Second, no one individual should monopolize the group. The delegation of functions and responsibilities should always have high priority. The enlistment of assistance from persons outside the immediate group should be undertaken in every area. Thus a local librarian or bookseller may be glad to help organize a parish library; someone on the local newspaper can help publicize some special event; and so forth. As we saw in considering church growth, the web of human associations can expand in many directions and by this means the parish as a whole maintains and extends its relation to the surrounding community.

Defining the Total Program

All of this leads to another consideration. An outward-looking group must be able to state what it stands for, clearly, simply, and honestly. A renewal group must formulate its goals in words. It is not enough to say that it desires to "improve the church," or "encourage education," or "be relevant." More specific and definable goals are essential. Yet, as we soon discover, renewal itself cannot be confined to any single area of parish life. There is little use in a fine church school for children if the ministry to teenagers and adults is so weak that most of the children sooner or later lapse. There is little point in an excellent program of stewardship if the money acquired thereby is wasted on elaborate, ornate, and little-used buildings. None of the individual areas for renewal can be ultimately satisfactory until related areas are also renewed. Renewal involves the revitalization of the whole scope of church life.

This is a simple but massive conclusion, and in the face of it, it is not surprising if many conclude that the task is hopeless. Yet this kind of strategic problem can in fact be met. The Associated Parishes, Inc., is a relatively small group of people who have for two decades been stimulating renewal in the Episcopal Church. This body has found this procedure to be the way to face the breadth of the problem. First, the group of persons concerned can make a list of all the different activities, concerns, and duties for which a parish ought to be responsible. These can then be grouped under major headings. These headings will include such topics as the following,[1] although the exact terms and manner of grouping may vary:

Worship
Pastoral care and ministry to people
Daily life and Christian witness of church members
Education
Social and community action
Evangelism, missions, and church extension
Ecumenism
The architectural and artistic witness of church buildings,
    music, and furnishings
Organization, administration, and finance

Every normal American congregation has a stake in every one of these areas, although different parishes differ greatly in the quantity and quality of their achievements under each heading, and perhaps no local church could be utterly effective in all these areas at once. Yet however much or little is presently being achieved in each area, the entire set of headings is in principle the total responsibility of every parish, and this can be clearly stated and understood. Having mapped out for itself a clear picture, a renewal group can plan its priorities, and over the course of several years it can devote some of its attention to each subject. Thus the members of the group acquaint themselves with the broad scope of the work of their local church, and in each area they can establish new personal contacts and involvements with persons interested in that particular area or field. Precisely because renewal is concerned with all these areas, what goes on in any one segment can be so planned as to strengthen what goes on in the other areas.

During a five- to ten-year period, a continuing goal of the renewal group can be to persuade the parish itself, through its clergy, its officers, vestry, trustees, or official board, to adopt a formal statement of the program of the parish in terms of every one of these major areas of responsibility, with some concrete and creative steps toward revitalization being specifically directed within each category. Thus, for example, under pastoral care and ministration, the standards for admitting adults to baptism can be spelled out, and the clergyman can thereafter uphold these standards with the knowledge that his people have faced the issues and will collectively support the decisions made. Similarly, in social action, the parish, rather than its pastor as an isolated figure, can bear its witness and can tell the community where it stands. Or under organization and administration, policies regarding assistant and self-supporting clergy can be defined, so that deacons or other nonstipendiary ministers can have recognized and mutually respectful relationships with the parish, on a basis which does not depend simply on the personal preferences of the senior clergyman or pastor. Of course every parish cannot fulfill every stipulation of a worthy and adequate parish program, but it can at least state its intentions and purposes.

Such a program can be outlined and printed, or reproduced by some method, and made readily available to everyone. Thus any man, woman, or child in the parish is equipped to tell a newcomer or an inquirer precisely *what this particular church is trying to do, and how it plans to do it.* Both the evangelist and the new member will be deeply grateful for this piece of basic equipment. When goals are clarified, meaningful ecumenical conversation with other Christians is much easier, and likewise with one's own denominational organizations. When the congregation knows what it is trying to do, it can think more seriously about its worship, for it is all this program which should be humbly but earnestly held up to God every Sunday, through the mediation of Jesus Christ, to be blessed and perfected by his Spirit. Since the Eucharist is the form of worship intended for this purpose, this service inevitably must hold a central place. Only a full liturgy of word and sacrament is adequate for a revitalized congregation.

Difficulties and Resources

No reader will suppose that all of this can be carried out in action as easily as it is printed on paper. In fact, innumerable problems will arise. Experiences of other people, however, helps us solve problems.

Most obvious is the problem of personnel. Most small congregations, and many larger ones, do not have men and women with the interest, background, or knowledge to make up even a small group to initiate a campaign for renewal. This problem may be met horizontally, ecumenically, vertically, and by church growth. By horizontally is meant reaching out to adjacent congregations in nearby communities. In a region characterized by small congregations or missions, it may take people drawn from three or four of these to form an effective cell. At the same time, it is increasingly realized that many of these things can be done in collaboration with members of other Christian bodies living in the same community. They frequently face the same problems, and as church members see how these problems arise in slightly different clothing in various churches, their own perception is sharpened and they learn to think and speak more clearly about basic issues. Ecumenicity itself is a goal of Christian renewal—here again the methods can bring the goal into sight. Especially important is the matter of objectivity. Members of the one congregation find it almost impossible to be objective when they alone speak together about controversial matters in the parish. We all tend to reduce everything to personal, emotional, and family loyalties or antipathies. The presence of outsiders forces us to frame our words and thoughts in broader, less personal terms. Unfamiliarity encourages respect, and people of any church certainly will be more polite and self-controlled when "outsiders" are present.

Third, there is the "vertical" dimension. National church organizations, as well as a variety of special societies and public agencies, have persons who are specifically equipped to discuss particular problems or fields of interest, and to train local persons to work in the field. A seriously concerned group of people can today easily secure some technical assistance in such diverse fields as summer camping for youngsters, care of alcoholics, or the improvement of church music. Fourth, all of this has a bearing on church growth. When serious and challenging projects are undertaken by people within a parish, they soon see the need of having enough people to implement their plans. Varying programs, some of which may be quite "secular" in their content, make the church better known and provide new contacts for potential growth in the surrounding community. Capable and responsible people, furthermore, are attracted to where the action is. Church groups that are doing a real job attract people who are able to do real jobs. One of the great thrills in the revitalization of religious life is to see the interested, capable, and creative people who emerge, even in an isolated and backward community where no such potentiality was believed to exist.

Another major problem is the pastoral one. Persons who start movements create problems—both for themselves and for others! When serious issues are aired, there will be disappointments and possibly quarrels. When constructive policies are formulated, officials and committee members who cannot implement these policies are forced out of office and their feelings are hurt. When new life brings in new membership, old members suspect that they are losing their grip and become depressed. The pastor will find that the demands made upon him are multiplied. As has been said before, the securing of assistant clergy, and the delegation of duties and responsibilities to clerical and lay assistants, are essential concerns. Furthermore, clergy, teachers, choir directors, and other people with specialized skills need new training from time to time to equip them for new tasks. Religious and secular agencies provide a variety of training conferences, summer schools, and so forth. It is important for lay people to encourage parish personnel to take advantage of such resources.

Another major obstacle may be described as administrative. A renewal group, or any other individuals, may conceive excellent plans, only to find them blocked by unsympathetic officials. If, let us say, a budget committee has funds which it will not release to the Sunday school for a much needed expenditure, it will do no good for persons interested in the Sunday school simply to complain. A better method is to make a list of the persons on the committee and then to ask someone known and respected by each committee member to contact the members and to explain the situation in a friendly and leisurely context. Our Lord carried out some of the most significant acts of his earthly ministry at meals: Christians need never be ashamed to use the dinner party as a means of propagating their ideas. When sufficient effort is made, agreements usually can be reached. In most church groups, it is procrastination rather than disagreement which is the enemy. People who have constructive and workable programs in mind, and who take reasonable and prompt steps to explain their position, usually can gain assent for their proposals.

What is said about administrative obstacles in a parish is equally true at the larger level of church organization. Many of the things discussed in this book—such as the ordination of local men who earn a living by secular work—will appear threatening to some officials and will accordingly be opposed or endlessly delayed. Here again those who have constructive proposals must make prompt and systematic efforts to establish friendly relations with those who are in decision-making positions. A small group of persons, who have enough conviction to keep promoting some policy over a period of years, can usually gain a fair hearing sooner or later—but woe to those who, when their chance comes, cannot explain themselves clearly or demonstrate a sufficient grasp of their own position!

A Renewal Group in Action

The unity of the various topics we have been considering can be seen in a specific example in which all these factors are operating. Let us take an issue not previously touched on.

Many people today are upset by current American attitudes and practices connected with death. Although much has recently been written on this subject, the average individual or family feels helpless and unable to promote any improvement, and so the subject embarrasses him and he prefers not to discuss it. Suppose a renewal group gives its attention to this topic. They will immediately discover that there are many puzzled but disquieted people who would support a constructive course of action if any were proposed. Clergy of all denominations will generally be glad to support steps to improve an area of their work which is often embarrassing and difficult for them. If several leading churches in an area will adopt certain agreed norms of practice, such decisions can be upheld. If undertakers, florists, and cemetery administrators are approached in a reasonable and constructive manner, they too will often be very helpful. In some communities, a substantial improvement can be effected and maintained.

Those who embark on this campaign will soon be exposed to all sorts of issues and new contacts. They will see the need of working with members of other churches. They will find how a wide variety of institutions and agencies are involved in maintaining or changing local customs and practices. They will discover how different sociological and ethnic groups have their own distinct ideas, some of which may be very commendable.

It will also be found that faults are not all on one side. The commercialization of death has filled a vacuum which churches, families, and public feeling have left untouched. What does the average parish do to inculcate better attitudes toward death? How is the communion of saints expressed in the normal round of weekly worship? What is done to clarify the relation of baptism and the Lord's Supper to death? These are indeed serious questions, and the concerned lay-man who has met with members of other churches, under-takers, and other persons of different backgrounds will be able to raise these questions in a more meaningful way within his own parish.

In the course of a year or two, some very substantial im-provements may have been introduced. Ecumenical links will have been made, and many interesting contacts around the community. Perhaps some permanent local board of clergy and morticians will be established, or a commission of the local Council of Churches appointed. At this point, the renewal group which initiated this campaign should with-draw. Continuing responsibility in relation to funerals can better be left in the hands of interested and qualified persons.

The group which is primarily concerned with Christian renewal should at once resume its normal round of prayer, study, and action in some other area. Perhaps the next year they will work to establish a chaplaincy in a local college, or enlist church support for soil and river conservation, or or-ganize a laymen's night school of theology. There is no end to things that can be done, and a group dedicated to renewal will seek to do them all under God's guidance. As has been said, such a group will make heavy demands on their pastor —but they should also expect him to equip himself, and plan his work, to meet such demands. Such a group will also make demands on the worship and sacramental life of their parishes because they will know that they need all the spiritual nurture they can get.

A striking ecumenical example of these things is provided in Washington, D.C., by the Church of the Saviour, under the leadership of the Rev. N. Gordon Cosby. This entire congregation conceives of itself as what we have called a renewal group. In order to become a member, one must first complete a substantial period of Christian training. One is then accepted for membership in the parish only if one demonstrates the capacity for sustained Christian witness and action. There are in fact far more applicants than can be accepted. This strongly motivated and disciplined group provides a far-reaching Christian ferment. Task forces made up of groups of members are constantly undertaking various projects in various parts of the city. Because the Church of the Saviour has no denominational affiliation, its position is unique and it will not, in this respect, be imitated by the average parish which rightly values its strong links with others whose faith and practice it shares. At the same time, however, the Church of the Saviour stands as a challenge to all denominations, and to all who say that such things cannot be done. Such things are being done on a large scale, even by very busy people in a very secular city. Any congregation can have a few people who are dedicated to Christian renewal.

After several years of initiating projects in a variety of areas—covering perhaps all of the headings of a basic parish program—members of a renewal group will have built up considerable competence. They will have faced a broad spectrum of spiritual, human, and practical problems. They will know their way around in many aspects of community life, and they will know how to find help in other areas. They will also learn how all of this can be nourished by constantly drawing on God's Word and sacraments and by constantly offering all successes and failures at his altar. Men and women who have engaged in this sort of thing during most of a decade will be mature Christians and, indeed, mature people. Among such people, a church can easily find men and women admirably equipped to undertake serious lay or ordained responsibilities with little or no further training. In this context, the training of deacons can virtually take care of itself. With a supply of mature leaders, churches can grow in numbers, and they can grow in strength.

How much can a church ask people to do? There is no one answer to the question, but those of us who have been engaged in this sort of thing know that a given individual can have a share in initiating some new activity or enterprise each year. In some cases it may be closely connected with professional interests, in other cases not. In some cases it may be a large project, in other cases a small one. In some cases it will require hours of hard work, and in other cases may require only the interest and conviction to give someone else the moral support they need at the right time. It is quite true that many churches do not encourage this sort of thing. It is quite true that many other lay people will be surprised and even indignant at a group of people who are avowedly trying to change both the church and the local community. Yet these things can be done, and when they are done followers will appear. Sometimes it may even happen that financial support is given.

Finally, the renewal of the Church is like the administration of baptism. It is an act of faith based on the certainty that God fulfills his promises. If Christians can be certain that God, the Father of Jesus Christ, is acting in us by his Holy Spirit, now, then we can look to the present and the future with hope and with joy. The Church can be young, in the assurance that this God is the one who makes all things new.

AUTHOR'S NOTES

Chapter 1: Church Growth Today

1. See memoir in *The Ministry of the Spirit,* ed. David M. Paton (Eerdmans, 1962).

2. *Missionary Methods: St. Paul's or Ours?* and *The Spontaneous Expansion of the Church,* both republished by Eerdmans (1962). *The Ministry of the Spirit,* mentioned above, is an anthology of Allen's writings and contains a condensation of his important work, *The Case for Voluntary Clergy. Missionary Principles* (Eerdmans, 1964) is a strong plea for missionary activity (conceived largely in terms of Asia and Africa) but is not so pertinent to our present study.

3. *The Bridges of God: A Study in the Strategy of Missions* (Friendship Press, 1955); *How Churches Grow: The New Frontier of Mission* (Friendship Press, 1959); (ed.) *Church Growth and Christian Mission* (Harper & Row, 1965).

4. *Christian Mass Movements in India* (Abingdon Press, 1933).

Chapter 2: Dimensions of Mission

1. José Ortega y Gasset, *The Revolt of the Masses* (25th Anniversary edition; Norton, 1957), pp. 11–12.

2. D. A. McGavran *The Bridges of God* (Friendship Press, 1955), chap. 2.

3. Many writers recognize the injustice of thus isolating a member of a minority group. See for instance *The Church in the Changing Community*, Publications in the Social Sciences, I (Fordham University Press, 1957), chap. 3.

4. Paul Tillich, *Theology of Culture* (Oxford University Press, 1959), p. 213.

Chapter 3: Extending the Ordained Ministry

1. The full original title of Roland Allen's second major work.

2. Roland Allen, *Missionary Methods* (Eerdmans, 1962), pp. 84f., 99ff.

3. Acts 18:2–3; 20:34; I Corinthians 9; I Thessalonians 2:9; II Thessalonians 3:8.

4. See Dr. Lukas Vischer, "The Ministry and a Secular Occupation" in *New Forms of Ministry*, ed., D. M. Paton (Edinburgh House, 1965).

5. See Peter Hammond, *The Waters of Marah: The Present State of the Greek Church* (Macmillan, 1956), for a good description of the system and for a striking brief biography (chap. 14) of a contemporary carpenter-priest. A vivid picture of a traditional Yugoslav parson is given in Ivo Andric, *Bridge on the Drina* (Macmillan, 1959), esp. chap. 10.

6. Douglas Webster, *Patterns of Part-Time Ministry* (World Dominion Press, 1964).

7. In *Church Growth and Christian Mission*, ed. Donald A. McGavran (Harper & Row, 1965), p. 191.

8. Among other literature, see Gregor Siefer, *The Church and Industrial Society* (Darton, Longman, and Todd, 1964); Henri Perrin, *Priest and Worker*, trans. B. Wall (Holt, Rinehart and Winston, 1964); *The Worker-Priests: A Collective Documentation*, trans. John Petrie (Routledge and Kegan Paul, 1956); *Priests and Workers: An Anglo-French Discussion*, ed., David L. Edwards (S.C.M. Press, 1961).

9. In *New Forms of Ministry*, ed. D. M. Paton, chap. V.

10. The reader of the Gospel in a High Mass is referred to as "the deacon," but he is normally in fact a priest.

11. *The Constitution on the Church* (*De ecclesia*), chap. III, 29. Available in various translations: e.g. Paulist Press edition (1965), pp. 122–123.

12. See P. Hammond, *The Waters of Marah* (Macmillan, 1956), pp. 36–37. For a less favorable view, *The Ministry of Deacons*, World Council Studies, No. 2, pp. 40–44.

13. *Ibid.*, pp. 58–71.

14. *Ibid.*, pp. 72–81.

15. *Ibid.*, pp. 54–57. In some parts of Scandinavia, the parish verger is called deacon. Elsewhere the term has been used for an assistant pastor.

16. *Ibid.*, pp. 45–53.

17. Canon 34, Sec. 10.

18. The legality and propriety of deacons carrying the consecrated elements of Holy Communion not only to the sick, but also to other individuals or groups who are isolated or impeded from attending normal public services, has recently been clarified and reaffirmed by the bishops of the Episcopal Church [*Minutes of*] *Special Meeting of House of Bishops*, Oct. 23–27, 1966.

19. Some proposals about the training of such men are given in the final chapter of this book.

20. The Rev. Paul Z. Hoornstra, Grace Church, Madison, Wisconsin.

21. For a helpful discussion of the entire subject, from the point of view of several different traditions, see *The Deaconess*, World Council of Churches Studies, No. 4.

22. See n. 21 above.

23. See Rajaiah D. Paul, *The First Decade: An Account of the Church of South India* (Christian Literature Society, 1958), pp. 146–151; *Empty Shoes: A Study of the Church of South India* (National Council of the Episcopal Church, 1956), pp. 77–81.

24. Some of these sisters were deaconesses in the mission churches prior to the union of the Church of South India.

25. For an interesting survey, see Olive Wyon, *Living Springs* (S.C.M. Press, 1963), chap. 3.

26. P. M. Dawley, *The Episcopal Church and Its Work* (Seabury Press, 1955), pp. 159–163.

27. L. G. Tyler, "One Hundred and Fifty Three," *Theology*, vol. lxiv (October, 1961), pp. 415–417.

28. Sydney Linton, "Swedish Statistics," *Prism*, No. 86 (June, 1964), pp. 10–13. This evidence indicates that the "strategy" of consolidation is seriously in error.

Chapter 4: The Evansville Associate Mission:
A Decade of Creativity

1. Moore studied at the Garret Biblical Institute and later at the Western Theological Seminary, both in Evanston. The latter institution merged a few years later with Seabury Divinity School (formerly in Faribault, Minnesota). He was ordained deacon, and later priest, by the Rt. Rev. Frank Arthur McElwain, Bishop of Minnesota. In Evanston he worked at St. Mark's Church.

2. For information regarding St. Paul's, I am much indebted to the present rector, the Rev. W. Robert Webb, and to a group of parishioners assembled by him to assist me with their reminiscences. Extensive information has also been contributed by the Rev. Dr. Imri M. Blackburn, Mrs. Anne K. Harris, Miss Juanita Spencer, and the Rev. John L. W. Thomas.

3. Moore's predecessor in the rectory was the Rev. E. Ainger Powell, who left Evansville in 1932 to become rector of Christ Church, Indianapolis.

4. Our study involves the area of Perry, Spencer, Warwick, Vanderburgh, Posey, and Gibson Counties.

5. Later ordained in Virginia.

6. This, and much other information, comes from unpublished recollections of Dr. Moore, compiled by Dr. Reuben Gross.

7. Active during the 1890's, this remarkable group included, among others, Irving P. Johnson, later Bishop of Colorado and editor of the *Witness*, and Paul Matthews, later Bishop of New Jersey.

8. See "Bishop's Annual Address," p. 28, *Journal*, Diocese of Indianapolis, 1935.

9. This and similar information may be confirmed in *The Clerical Directory*, published in New York every three years.

10. Located not far from Evansville, this is an important Benedictine center.

11. For information and assistance when visiting Mount Vernon, I am much indebted to the vicar, the Rev M. A. McClure. For details regarding churches in all these towns, the successive editions of the *Episcopal Church Annual*, published in New York, and its predecessor, the *Living Church Annual*, are most helpful.

12. For information and assistance when visiting New Harmony, my thanks are due to the vicar, the Rev. Arthur C. Hadley, and Mrs. Kenneth Dale Owen. There is an extensive published literature on this remarkable community.

13. The Rev. C. H. McKnight left in September, 1932, after staying "seven years to the day" (unpublished parish memoirs of Mrs. Elsie W. Overstreet). The Rev. Charles E. Howe arrived as a deacon in 1933 and was ordained a priest at New Harmony. In 1934 he was unfortunately forced by ill health to go to Arizona, where his subsequent ministry has been exercised.

14. For information and assistance when visiting Cannelton, my gratitude is due to the vicar, the Rev. John G. Barrow.

15. Immediately prior to our period, it was served by the Rev. R. A. Crickmer, rector of St. Paul's, Jeffersonville, sixty miles or more to the east (immediately across the Ohio River from Louisville). An older man, he cannot have found it easy to make this trip often, especially on Sunday morning. With his retirement in 1934, this arrangement had to be terminated, and Jeffersonville remained dependent for some years on supply clergy from Indianapolis.

16. Later ordained in Minnesota.

17. Moore attributes this arrangement to the influence of the Rev. George Craig Steward, then rector of St. Luke's Church, Evanston, Illinois, and later Bishop of Chicago.

18. Excerpts from the parish records kindly supplied by Miss Juanita Spencer. Things in fact worked out somewhat differently (as they often did), and O'Brien did not reside at Good Shepherd.

19. Father O'Brien has subsequently served in central New York.

20. I am indebted to him for information regarding the parish during this period.

21. In his graduate studies and subsequently, Dr. Moore has carried on remarkable research into the folk religions of Jamaica. In this field he has found dramatic evidence of the ability of poor and uneducated people to produce their own dynamic religious leadership.

Chapter 5: Worship in a Living Church

1. Besides the second chapter of I Peter, the doctrine of the royal priesthood appears in Exodus 19:6; Isaiah 61:6; and Revelation 1:6; 5:10.

2. This is ultimately true both of the Western Apostles' Creed and of the Eastern Nicene Creed. See J.N.D. Kelly, *Early Christian Creeds* (2nd ed.; Longmans, 1960).

3. The Eastern Churches still follow the ancient custom of commemorating this event on Epiphany. In the Western liturgical tradition, it is commemorated shortly after Epiphany and receives little emphasis.

4. J. G. Davies, *The Architectural Setting of Baptism* (Barrie and Rockliff, 1962).

5. The assigning of this role to the bishop will be found regularly in ancient liturgical documents.

6. This is the official view of the Anglican Church. See Book of Common Prayer (current U.S. ed.), p. 279.

7. Ascension Day (presumably in the evenings) and the Sunday between Ascension and Pentecost are highly suitable for baptism and confirmation, and in most parts of the United States, in many years, they come late enough in the spring for outdoor baptisms. The Sunday after Pentecost, Trinity Sunday,

is again obviously appropriate for baptism in the Triune Name and for the rites which follow it. The patronal feasts of some parishes likewise occur in the summer and provide auspicious dates for bringing new members into the Body of Christ.

8. H. B. Porter, *The Day of Light* (Seabury Press, 1960).

9. St. Augustine's Episcopal Church, Washington, D.C., exercised widespread influence during several years when it worshiped in a restaurant every Sunday morning.

10. The earliest and perhaps still the clearest description of this pattern is that written in Rome about A.D. 150 by St. Justin Martyr; see his *First Apology*, chap. 67 (many editions and translations).

11. *The Book of Common Worship* (Oxford University Press, 1963), pp. 5–20. The rite was earlier published in pamphlet form.

12. *The Eucharistic Liturgy of Taizé*, trans. John Arnold (Canterbury Press, 1962).

13. Among the various editions, convenient pamphlet texts of the English translation of *The Constitution on the Sacred Liturgy* were published by the Liturgical Press (1963) and by the Paulist Press (1964).

14. For an excellent presentation of the Roman Mass as performed on Sundays in American parishes, see *The Book of Catholic Worship*, published by the Liturgical Conference (1966). Note especially pp. xvii–xx and 383–388.

15. For an example representing eight Lutheran churches in America, see *Service Book and Hymnal*, published by several Lutheran church houses, 1958 music edition, pp. 1–14.

16. For example, *Service for the Lord's Day* (Westminster Press, 1964), Presbyterian Church in the U.S. and the United Presbyterian Church in the U.S.A.

17. For an example from the Christian Church (Disciples of Christ), see Keith Watkins, *The Breaking of Bread* (Bethany Press, 1966).

18. In U.S.A., *The Liturgy of the Lord's Supper* (Church Pension Fund, 1966). For a foreign example, *The Liturgy or Eucharist of the Church of the Province of New Zealand* (Association of

Anglican Bookrooms, 1966). For unofficial English proposal, G. D. Kilpatrick, *Remaking the Liturgy* (Fontana Library, 1967).

19. Much information and an extensive recent bibliography of works pertaining to liturgical renewal will be found in *The Liturgical Movement and the Local Church*, by Alfred E. Shands. 2nd ed., Morehouse-Barlow, 1965.

20. Reginald H. Fuller, *What Is Liturgical Preaching?* (Allenson, 1957).

Chapter 6: Starting Today

1. See *A Parish Program for Liturgy and Mission* (Associated Parishes, Inc., 116 West Washington Avenue, Madison, Wisconsin). This agency also publishes other material pertinent to the renewal of the local church.